Mark Twain

Mark Twain

MARK TWAIN

by Nancy Skarmeas

IDEALS PUBLICATIONS INCORPORATED

NASHVILLE, TENNESSEE

ISBN 0-8249-4085-7

Printed and bound in the U.S.A. by
R. R. Donnelley & Sons, Roanoke, Virginia.

Library of Congress Cataloging-in-Publication Data
Mark Twain. -- 1st ed.
        p. cm. -- (Great Americans)
  Includes bibliographical references and index.
  ISBN 0-8249-4085-7 (alk. paper)
  1. Twain, Mark, 1835–1910. 2. Authors, American--19th century-
-Biography. 3. Twain, Mark, 1835–1910--Quotations. I. Twain,
Mark, 1835–1910. Selections. 1998. II. Ideals Publications
Incorporated. III. Series: Great Americans (Nashville, Tenn.)
PS1331.M215 1998
818'.409--dc21
[b]   98-7980
                                       CIP

First Edition
10 8 6 4 2 1 3 5 7 9

Publisher and Editor: Patricia A. Pingry
Associate Editor: Michelle Prater Burke
Designer: Eve DeGrie
Copy Editor: Kristi Richardson
Editorial Assistant: Christine Landry

Color Film Separations by Precision Color Graphics,
New Berlin, Wisconsin.

Published by Ideals Publications Incorporated
535 Metroplex Drive, Suite 250
Nashville, TN 37211

Art on cover (*detail*) and page 82 (*in full*):
Portrait of Mark Twain by Frank Edwin Larson.
National Portrait Gallery, Washington, D.C.

Smithsonian Institution/Art Resource, NY.
Photo on cover, half-title and page 28: Archive Photos.
Art on the preceding pages:
JOLLY FLATBOATMEN IN PORT, 1857
George Caleb Bingham (1811–1879)
Oil on Canvas
47 1/16 x 69 5/8 inches
The St. Louis Art Museum
Museum Purchase
St. Louis, Missouri.
Photo page 8: Ideals Publications Incorporated.
Photo page 20: SuperStock.
Photo page 44: Mark Twain Memorial, Hartford, CT/SuperStock.
Photo page 70: The Mark Twain House.
Mark Twain's signature: The Mark Twain House.

We are greatly indebted to Britt Barry, Director of Education for Public Programs, The Mark Twain House, Hartford, Connecticut, for her invaluable assistance. We send a special thanks also to all those at The Mark Twain House for their help in the photographic research for this book and in their encouragement throughout the project.

ACKNOWLEDGMENTS

Clemens, Clara. Two excerpts from MY FATHER MARK TWAIN, copyright © 1931 by Clara Clemens Gabrilowitsch, renewed © 1958 by Clara Clemens Samossound. Reprinted by permission of HarperCollins Publishers, Inc. Condon, Garret. An excerpt from the article "Typesetter Misses Deadline for Success" from THE HARTFORD COURANT. Reprinted with the permission of THE HARTFORD COURANT. Kaplan, Justin. Excerpts from MR. CLEMENS AND MARK TWAIN. Copyright © 1966 by Justin Kaplan. Excerpts from MARK TWAIN AND HIS WORLD. Copyright © 1974 by George Rainbird Ltd. Both reprinted with the permission of Simon & Schuster. Lennon, Nigey. Excerpts from MARK TWAIN IN CALIFORNIA, copyright © 1982, 1998, Nigey Lennon. Reprinted by permission of the author. Neider, Charles, editor. Six excerpts from THE AUTOBIOGRAPHY OF MARK TWAIN, copyright © 1917, 1940, 1958, 1959 by The Mark Twain Company, renewed 1987. Copyright © 1924, 1945, 1952 by Clara Clemens Samossound. Copyright ©1959 by Charles Neider, renewed 1987. Reprinted by permission of HarperCollins Publishers, Inc. Additional territory granted by Curtis Brown, Ltd. Sanborn, Margaret. Excerpts from MARK TWAIN: THE BACHELOR YEARS, copyright © 1990 by Margaret Sanborn. Used by permission of the author, Mill Valley, CA. Twain, Mark. The Mark Twain Project. MARK TWAIN'S LETTERS, VOLUME 1: 1853–1866, ed. Edgar Marquess Branch, Michael B. Frank, Kenneth M. Sanderson, Harriet Elinor Smith, Lin Salamo, and Richard Bucci, 1988. MARK TWAIN'S LETTERS, VOLUME 2: 1867–1868, ed. Harriet Elinor Smith, Richard Bucci, and Lin Salamo, 1990. Both from THE MARK TWAIN PAPERS, Berkeley, Los Angeles, and London: University of California Press.

CONTENTS

PREFACE

Born in a tiny village near the Mississippi River in 1835, Samuel Langhorne Clemens grew up at the crossroads of young America. He began his life in Hannibal, Missouri, where pioneers trekking westward crossed paths with steamboats traveling north and south on the great river that divided the nation between the settled East and the frontier West. All this movement proved irresistible to Clemens, a boy with energy and imagination to spare; and, at an early age, he set out to see the world. In the years to come, he was a printer, a riverboat pilot, a Civil War soldier, a prospector, a miner, and a frontier journalist before he discovered his talent for writing fiction and began to create, under the name Mark Twain, the novels and stories that would make him famous.

Nearly a century after the death of Sam Clemens, Mark Twain remains ubiquitous in American culture. Students from elementary school to graduate school read and study his novels; journalists regularly quote his words; advertisers promote their products with his image; television programs have been known to write him in as a character; schools, banks and restaurants bear his name; and two of his fictional characters—Tom Sawyer and Huck Finn—have leaped off the pages of his novels to achieve a mythic life of their own in American culture. Yet in spite of Twain's ubiquitousness, or perhaps because of it, too many Americans take him, and his creator Clemens, for granted. So familiar is Mark Twain that we simply assume that we know him. However, Samuel Clemens has never been an easy man to know.

One of Clemens's closest friends, the novelist and editor William Dean Howells, once commented on the lingering mystery of the man. "You were all there for him," Howells said, "but he was not all there for you." Howells's words ring true. Clemens's life was full of contradictions. As an adult, he settled in Hartford, Connecticut, worlds away from his Missouri roots; but he found his creative energies constantly pulling him back to the Mississippi River of his childhood. He decried capitalism and the curse of greed, yet he married into enormous wealth, befriended great industrialists, and schemed all his life, albeit unsuccessfully, to make a fortune of his own. Even his writing was based upon a contradiction. Clemens wrote with brilliant humor about questions and issues that filled him with anger, disgust, and despair. Behind the character of Mark Twain—the master storyteller who aimed only to

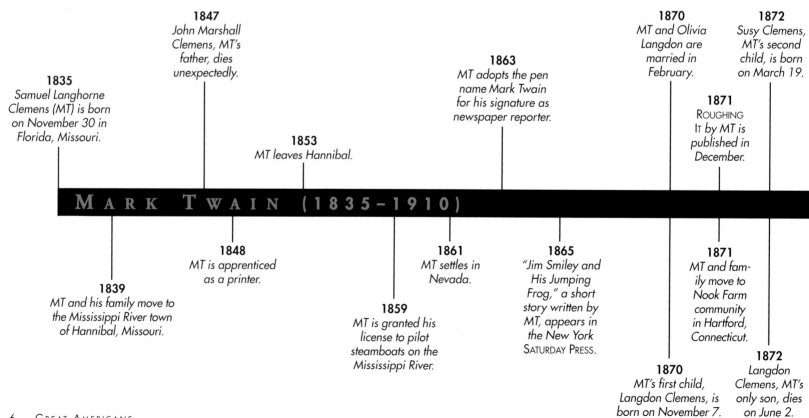

1835
Samuel Langhorne Clemens (MT) is born on November 30 in Florida, Missouri.

1839
MT and his family move to the Mississippi River town of Hannibal, Missouri.

1847
John Marshall Clemens, MT's father, dies unexpectedly.

1848
MT is apprenticed as a printer.

1853
MT leaves Hannibal.

1859
MT is granted his license to pilot steamboats on the Mississippi River.

1861
MT settles in Nevada.

1863
MT adopts the pen name Mark Twain for his signature as newspaper reporter.

1865
"Jim Smiley and His Jumping Frog," a short story written by MT, appears in the New York SATURDAY PRESS.

1870
MT and Olivia Langdon are married in February.

1870
MT's first child, Langdon Clemens, is born on November 7.

1871
ROUGHING IT by MT is published in December.

1871
MT and family move to Nook Farm community in Hartford, Connecticut.

1872
Susy Clemens, MT's second child, is born on March 19.

1872
Langdon Clemens, MT's only son, dies on June 2.

MARK TWAIN (1835–1910)

amuse—lurked Clemens, who was more preacher than humorist. Indeed, he used humor as a weapon. "Against the assault of laughter," he wrote, "nothing can stand."

Out of this maze of contradictions emerged one of the most skilled, insightful, and influential writers America has ever known. Clemens, as Mark Twain, freed American fiction from the heavy shadow of European culture and turned its energies toward the rich variety of American customs, dialects, and cultures he had absorbed in the travels and experiences of his youth. Ernest Hemingway once wrote that "all modern American literature comes from one book by Mark Twain called *Huckleberry Finn*." This is not hyperbole. Displaying an uncanny grasp of the vernacular of the Mississippi River area, Twain became the boy Huck, using that unforgettable voice to reveal both the wonderful potential and the frightening prejudices that characterized the American nation in the middle of the nineteenth century. Beginning with *ADVENTURES OF HUCKLEBERRY FINN*, the American character became a legitimate subject for serious literature, and Mark Twain became celebrated the world over as *the* American author.

In the pages that follow are assembled an eclectic collection of words and images that document the life and times of Samuel Langhorne Clemens. The author himself left an amazing wealth of material

for biographers. He wrote novels, plays, science fiction, history, social satire, and more. He gave countless speeches, wrote essays on politics, and was a dependable correspondent. He also dictated, in the last months of his life, a fascinating, rambling stream of autobiographical material that is still challenging biographers bent on publishing a definitive edition. The task of selecting a handful of excerpts from this vast library has been daunting. Clemens was truly a man larger than life, a man difficult to reduce to the limits of a slim volume. Yet his own words reprinted here—excerpts from his autobiography, from his major novels and stories, from his letters and speeches—and enriched by the words of the best of his many biographers, of friends that knew him, of family members that loved him, of critics and commentators who watched him perform on life's great stage, do present a full if not a complete portrait of a many-sided man. With photos from both his public and private lives, illustrations from his novels, and art that captures the spirit of the era, this volume reaches beyond the familiar image of Mark Twain to offer a glimpse of Samuel Clemens, a man of true genius and insight, a man who understood America far better than it ever understood him, and who gave an authentic literary voice to a nation struggling to come of age in the world.

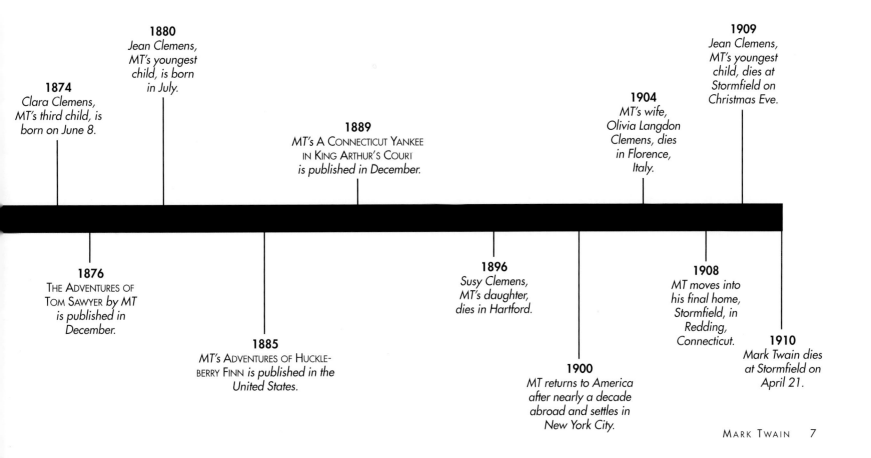

1874
Clara Clemens, MT's third child, is born on June 8.

1880
Jean Clemens, MT's youngest child, is born in July.

1889
MT's A CONNECTICUT YANKEE IN KING ARTHUR'S COURT *is published in December.*

1904
MT's wife, Olivia Langdon Clemens, dies in Florence, Italy.

1909
Jean Clemens, MT's youngest child, dies at Stormfield on Christmas Eve.

1876
THE ADVENTURES OF TOM SAWYER *by MT is published in December.*

1885
MT's ADVENTURES OF HUCKLEBERRY FINN *is published in the United States.*

1896
Susy Clemens, MT's daughter, dies in Hartford.

1900
MT returns to America after nearly a decade abroad and settles in New York City.

1908
MT moves into his final home, Stormfield, in Redding, Connecticut.

1910
Mark Twain dies at Stormfield on April 21.

Mark Twain

MISSISSIPPI BOYHOOD
1835–1853

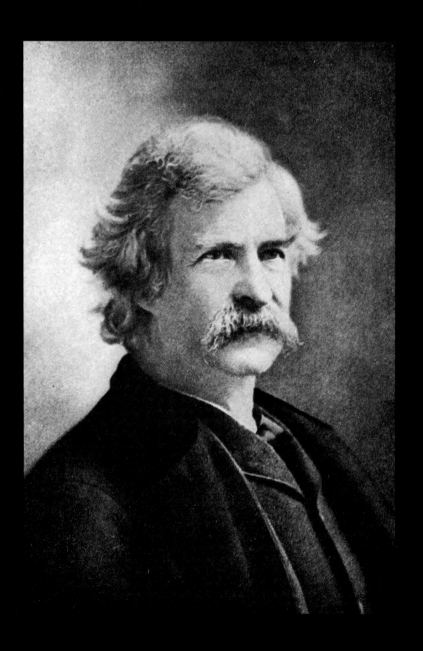

Samuel Langhorne Clemens entered the world in the tiny northeastern Missouri village of Florida on November 30, 1835. There were twenty-four states in the union, the country's population stood at seven million, and Halley's comet was visible—although dim and unspectacular—in the night skies. John Marshall and Jane Lampton Clemens held out little hope for their son, a sickly, premature infant who was not expected to survive his first winter. But Samuel was there to see the spring, and there four years later when the Clemens family packed up and moved to the nearby Mississippi River town of Hannibal. Situated on the edge of the frontier, at the gateway to the American West, Hannibal was a growing and thriving hub for a nation in motion: steamboats crowded the river moving passengers and cargo north and south; wagons and horses carried pioneers and prospectors along Hannibal's streets on their way to the promised land in the West. Young Sam Clemens absorbed every ounce of the rich and compelling romance of life on the Mississippi. He dreamed of piloting a riverboat, of exploring the world, of striking gold in California. He did not, by any indications, dream of becoming an author; but when he left Hannibal in 1853, Clemens took with him a treasure chest of stories of river life and river people that one day, as the writer Mark Twain, he would transform into magical works of fiction.

Illustration at right by Norman Rockwell from THE ADVENTURES OF TOM SAWYER, *1936 edition.*

FAMILY BACKGROUNDS

FROM *MARK TWAIN AND HIS WORLD*, BY JUSTIN KAPLAN

1835

Samuel Langhorne Clemens (MT) is born on November 30 in Florida, Missouri, to Jane Lampton Clemens and John Marshall Clemens.

1835

French writer Alexis de Tocqueville examines the American system of government in his classic work DEMOCRACY IN AMERICA.

1836

Ralph Waldo Emerson publishes NATURE and joins with Nathaniel Hawthorne, Henry David Thoreau, and other authors and philosophers to form the Transcendentalist Club.

1837

Financial panic occurs when New York banks refuse to make payouts in gold or silver. Economic depression and widespread unemployment follow.

1837

Samuel F. Morse applies for a patent on the telegraph.

1838

Fourteen thousand Cherokee Indians are forcibly marched out of Georgia to reservation land in Oklahoma. The march, known as the Trail of Tears, is part of the federal government's plan to move all native Americans to land west of the Mississippi River. Four thousand Cherokee men, women, and children die during the march.

1839

The abolitionist Liberty Party holds its first national convention in Warsaw, New York, to select candidates for the upcoming American presidential election.

Samuel Clemens's mother, Jane Lampton Clemens, was an affectionate, optimistic, funny woman with a flair for storytelling and a distinctive drawl to her speech. His father, John Marshall Clemens, a lawyer, judge, justice of the peace, and sometime businessman, was by all accounts a hard-working and well-respected man; but he nonetheless struggled to keep financially afloat throughout his adult life and never allowed himself to be affectionate or soft with his children. The story is told by many biographers that Jane made Sam pledge as a young boy that he would be as somber and industrious as his father. Whether or not the instruction was ever given, Clemens's life and career offer indisputable proof that it was not heeded. In this excerpt from MARK TWAIN AND HIS WORLD, Justin Kaplan describes the family into which Samuel Langhorne Clemens was born.

In 1823 John Marshall Clemens, lawyer and storekeeper, settled with his bride, Jane Lampton, in Columbia, Kentucky. They had a common background: their families had been slaveholders and small landowners in the South, poor gentry, but gentry nevertheless; and, as Mark Twain was to recall with some amusement, his parents were Virginians and ancestor-proud. Marshall Clemens (named, in a hopeful mood, after the Virginian who was to become Chief Justice of the Supreme Court) was descended from one of the regicide judges who sent King Charles I of England to the headsman's block, while the Lamptons grandly traced their connection to the earls of Durham and even considered taking steps to claim the title when it fell vacant. Although he was to ridicule the whole title business, Mark Twain entertained himself from time to time with a fantasy that he had become Earl of Durham, wrote a novel called *The American Claimant*, and had a lifelong passion for claimants of all sorts. . . .

Jane Clemens in her eighties said that she had married "in a pet," to spite another man, and whether this was truth or imagining, it still suggests that although they were well matched in background Mark Twain's father and mother were at best not wholly compatible throughout their twenty-four years together. In character and personality they were antithetic. Play, humor, laughter, tenderness—Mark Twain saw these chiefly in his mother. "She was of a sunshiny disposition, and her long life was mainly a holiday to her," he wrote. "She always had the heart of a young girl." Through all the family troubles she maintained a kind of perky stoicism, which was lightened considerably by her love for gossip, gaudy spectacles like parades and funerals, bright colors, and animals.

But Mark Twain described his father as "stern, unsmiling, never demonstrated affection for wife or child. . . . Silent, austere, of perfect probity and high principle; ungentle of manner toward his children, but always a gentleman in his phrasing—and never punished them—a look was enough, and more than enough. . . . It was remembered that he went to church—once; never again." . . .

Dreaming of great riches and also haunted by a fear of sinking in the world, Marshall Clemens invested his hopes and his assets in what turned out to be a series of disasters. He left

Kentucky and moved to Fentress County, Tennessee, where he eventually acquired about seventy thousand acres of virgin land. He expected to become rich on the coal, copper, and iron ore that supposedly lay in the soil where potatoes and wild grass were growing. In this expectation, which never panned out in his or his children's lifetime, he laid upon the shoulders of the Clemens family what Mark Twain called the heavy curse of prospective wealth: "It is good to begin life poor; it is good to begin life rich—these are wholesome; but to begin it poor and *prospectively* rich! The man who has not experienced it cannot imagine the curse of it."

Meanwhile, in search of more immediate rewards, Marshall Clemens followed the tide of settlement across the Mississippi into Missouri where he became a storekeeper in the crossroads hamlet of Florida. It was there, on 30 November 1835, that Jane Clemens gave birth to the sixth of their seven children, Samuel, named after his paternal grandfather. Halley's comet blazed in the night sky when he was born, just as it would when he died in April 1910. By then, "light years" removed from Florida, he had come to think of himself and the comet as "unaccountable freaks" who, since they had come in together, "must go out together."

Marshall Clemens became a county judge in Florida but failed to make a go of it as storekeeper, and in 1839 he moved his family for the last time, forty miles east to the Mississippi, to Hannibal. There, in addition to seeking a living from several mercantile ventures, none of which thrived, he served as justice of the peace, practicing attorney, president of the Library Association, and chairman of the Committee on Roads. He was accounted one of the first citizens of the town. Even so, until he died in 1847 at the age of forty-nine, Judge Clemens continued to follow his fading star into poverty, dispossession, bankruptcy, exhaustion, and hopelessness. He had failed in the law, in business, in land speculation, and even in a venture or two in slave trading. . . .

These were some of the family backgrounds of Mark Twain, who all his life hungered for affection. He was capable of great rage and greater remorse, and was sometimes like a child demanding attention and approval in a nursery as big as the world. He could never separate the idyl of boyhood from the terror. And as a miner in the West, and later as businessman, speculator, and publisher caught up in the scramble of the Gilded Age, he repeated his father's pattern—he lived in dread of debt but within sight of enormous prospective wealth, and he went broke.

Much of Mark Twain's public persona traces easily back to Jane Clemens, above, the devoted mother who guided her son through his active and mischievous youthful days. Shortly after his mother's death, Clemens wrote a tribute to her titled simply, "Jane Lampton Clemens." The sentimental piece remained unpublished until Clemens's first biographer, Albert Bigelow Paine, inserted it into the 1924 edition of MARK TWAIN'S AUTOBIOGRAPHY. Photo The Mark Twain Papers.

John Marshall Clemens died when Samuel was only eleven, but he left an indelible impression on his son's imagination. At least two of the characters of Mark Twain's fiction—TOM SAWYER and HUCK FINN's Judge Thatcher as well as PUD-DN'HEAD WILSON's Judge Driscoll—are believed to have been based primarily on John Marshall Clemens. In THE INNOCENTS ABROAD, Twain tells a story about visiting his father's law office, pictured at right, in the middle of the night and coming upon the body of a murder victim. Photo The Mark Twain House and Joseph Farber.

A CHILD'S MEMORY

FROM *THE AUTOBIOGRAPHY OF MARK TWAIN*, EDITED BY CHARLES NEIDER

1839

John Marshall Clemens, MT's father, sells his home and land in Florida and moves his family east to the Mississippi River town of Hannibal, where he hopes to cash in on the growing town's booming river economy. MT is four years old.

1839

Theodore Dwight Weld, a Massachusetts abolitionist, publishes AMERICAN SLAVERY AS IT IS, which uses reports from Southern newspapers as well as eyewitness accounts and the testimony of former slaves to depict the horror of slavery in the United States. The book is extremely influential and wins many converts to the abolitionist cause. Author Harriet Beecher Stowe later credits Weld's book as the inspiration for her novel UNCLE TOM'S CABIN.

1841

The first covered wagon train to California leaves northeastern Kansas in May. The settlers will reach Sonora, California, by November.

1840

MT begins school in Hannibal at the home of Mrs. Elizabeth Horr, the wife of a local cooper and a native of New York City.

1842

John C. Frémont begins his exploration of the Rocky Mountains as America's westward movement continues.

1843

More than one thousand settlers leave Independence, Missouri in May on their way to Oregon. Traveling by covered wagon, they arrive in Oregon in five months.

1843

A primitive version of the typewriter is invented in Worcester, Massachusetts; the invention is not made truly efficient, however, until 1867.

Clemens devoted the last years of his life to dictating material for his autobiography, and editors have spent the ensuing century trying to publish a definitive version of the work. The task is a daunting, if not impossible, one. As the excerpt below shows, Clemens's style was haphazard and rambling, with little regard to matters of chronology or organization. Charles Neider was the third editor to attempt to impose form on Clemens's voluminous autobiographical material. In the text below, Clemens begins speaking of his birth and ends with an anecdote given to prove the unreliability of the speaker's own memory for matters of fact.

I was born the 30th of November, 1835, in the almost invisible village of Florida, Monroe County, Missouri. My parents removed to Missouri in the early 'thirties; I do not remember just when, for I was not born then and cared nothing for such things. It was a long journey in those days and must have been a rough and tiresome one. The village contained a hundred people and I increased the population by 1 per cent. It is more than many of the best men in history could have done for a town. It may not be modest in me to refer to this but it is true. There is no record of a person doing as much—not even Shakespeare. But I did it for Florida and it shows that I could have done it for any place—even London, I suppose.

Recently some one in Missouri has sent me a picture of the house I was born in. Heretofore I have always stated that it was a palace but I shall be more guarded now.

The village had two streets, each a couple of hundred yards long; the rest of the avenues mere lanes, with rail fences and cornfields on either side. Both the streets and the lanes were paved with the same material—tough black mud in wet times, deep dust in dry.

Most of the houses were of logs—all of them, indeed, except three or four; these latter were frame ones. There were none of brick and none of stone. There was a log church, with a puncheon floor and slab benches. A puncheon floor is made of logs whose upper surfaces have been chipped flat with the adz. The cracks between the logs were not filled; there was no carpet; consequently, if you dropped anything smaller than a peach it was likely to go through. The church was perched upon short sections of logs, which elevated it two or three feet from the ground. Hogs slept under there, and whenever the dogs got after them during services the minister had to wait till the disturbance was over. In winter there was always a refreshing breeze up through the puncheon floor; in summer there were fleas enough for all. . . .

There were two stores in the village. My uncle, John A. Quarles, was proprietor of one of them. It was a very small establishment, with a few rolls of "bit" calicoes on half a dozen shelves; a few barrels of salt mackerel, coffee and New Orleans sugar behind the counter; stacks of brooms, shovels, axes, hoes, rakes and such things here and there; a lot of cheap hats, bonnets and tinware strung on strings and suspended from the walls; and at the other end of the room was another counter with bags of shot on it, a cheese or two and a keg of powder; in front of it a row of nail kegs and a few pigs of lead, and behind it a barrel or two of New Orleans molasses and native corn whisky on tap. If a boy bought five or ten cents' worth of anything he was entitled to half a handful of sugar from the barrel; if a woman bought a few yards of calico she was entitled to a spool of thread in addition to the usual gratis "trimmin's"; if a man bought a trifle he was at liberty to draw and swallow as big a drink of whisky as he wanted. . . .

At first my father owned slaves but by and by he sold them and hired others by the year from the farmers. For a girl of fifteen he paid twelve dollars a year and gave her two lin-sey-woolsey frocks and a pair of "stogy" shoes—cost, a modification of nothing; for a negro woman of twenty-five, as general house servant, he paid twenty-five dollars a year and gave her shoes and the aforementioned linsey-woolsey frocks; for a strong negro woman of forty, as cook, washer, etc., he paid forty dollars a year and the customary two suits of clothes; and for an able-bodied man he paid from seventy-five to a hundred dollars a year and gave him two suits of jeans and two pairs of "stogy" shoes—an outfit that cost about three dollars.

I used to remember my brother Henry walking into a fire outdoors when he was a week old. It was remarkable in me to remember a thing like that and it was still more remark-able that I should cling to the delusion for thirty years that I *did* remember it—for of course it never happened; he would not have been able to walk at that age. If I had stopped to reflect I should not have burdened my memory with that impossible rubbish so long. It is believed by many people that an impression deposited within a child's memory within the first two years of its life cannot remain there five years but that is an error. The incident of Benvenuto Cellini and the salamander must be accepted as authentic and trustworthy; and then that remarkable and indisputable instance in the experience of Helen Keller. For many years I believed that I remembered helping my grandfather drink his whiskey toddy when I was six weeks old but I do not tell about that any more now; I am grown old and my memory is not as active as it used to be. When I was younger I could remember anything, whether it had happened or not; but my faculties are decaying now and soon I shall be so I cannot remember any but the things that never happened. . . .

Henry Clemens, above, born in 1838, three years after his brother Samuel, was the youngest of the Clemens children. Sam and Henry enjoyed the special relationship of close brothers: they played together, fought together, and remained loyal to each other until the end. Henry died tragically before he reached the age of twenty in circumstances that were forever to haunt his brother. After beginning his own career as a steamboat pilot, Sam urged Henry to join him on the river and, in 1858, found him a place as a mud clerk on a ship called the PENNSYLVANIA. Following a run-in with the pilot, Sam Clemens left the boat, and shortly thereafter it suffered a massive explosion. Sam rushed back to be with his brother, but Henry died in his arms. Forever after, Clemens blamed himself for his brother's death, and his memories of his brother were always burdened by a painful guilt. Photo The Mark Twain House.

Orion Clemens, left, was Sam's oldest brother and, after the death of their father in 1847, the head of the family. Orion worked as a printer, a journalist, an editor, and a minor government official; and, after his younger brother's success as a writer brought him some financial stability, he tried his hand at law, farming, writing, and inventing. In many ways Orion was like his father—an intelligent, hard-working man who nonetheless found it hard to achieve any stability or financial security in his life. Sam often expressed disbelief and disappointment at his brother's actions; he variously described his brother as volatile, weak-minded, and a dreamer. In his autobiography, he calls Orion "the strangest compound that ever got mixed in a human mold." Photo The Mark Twain House.

AN UNCERTAIN CHILD

FROM *MARK TWAIN: THE BACHELOR YEARS,* BY MARGARET SANBORN

Biographer Margaret Sanborn, whose book details Clemens's life up until his marriage in 1870, describes below an exchange between Sam and his mother that reveals their common love of and flair for the dramatic, and also gives credence to the many legends of Clemens's wild and unruly boyhood.

The Clemens family arrived in the village of Florida about the first of June 1835. Shortly, John Marshall rented the two-room frame house on South Mill Street, just a few doors away from the store of his brother-in-law, John Quarles. Until he could set up a law practice, Clemens went into partnership with him. Then, applying his formula for success, he plunged into the purchase of land, making down-payments on a 120-acre tract of government land east of town, and on eighty acres of timber. In September, he bought a three-acre parcel on North Mill Street and began planning a house that would be in keeping with his social position.

On November 30, Jane Lampton unexpectedly went into labor and Dr. Thomas Jefferson Chowning, yet another Virginian, was called in to deliver the premature boy, whom they named Samuel Langhorne. Nothing was ready. There was not even a shirt to put on the child, but neighbors came to the rescue with used baby clothes.

It is curious that John Marshall agreed to name his son for the father against whom he still held a grudge, but he doubtless thought it mattered little for it seemed obvious the boy would not live long.

Jane succeeded in pulling Sam through that crucial first winter, but he remained a "sickly and precarious and tiresome and uncertain child" until he was eight years old, and always more trouble than the rest of Jane's brood collectively. Once, after he was grown, he was talking with his mother about those early years, and asked, "I suppose that during all that time you were uneasy about me?"

"Yes, the whole time."

"Afraid I wouldn't live?"

Then, after a pause designed to give impact to the kind of remark they both relished, "No—afraid you would."

HANNIBAL, ON THE MISSISSIPPI

FROM "THE BOYHOOD HOME OF MARK TWAIN," BY HENRY M. WHARTON

The town of Hannibal shaped Sam Clemens's childhood; as an adult, Clemens would repay the favor by reshaping his hometown in the fictional works of Mark Twain. The Hannibal that appears in THE ADVENTURES OF TOM SAWYER *under the name of St. Petersburg is an idealized and simplified version of the author's hometown and certainly bears only a slight resemblance to the Hannibal of Twain's publishing days. The convergence of three railroad lines and a booming lumber industry had transformed Hannibal, increasing the population tenfold since the year the Clemens family arrived there. Articles like the one below, taken from a 1902 edition of* CENTURY *magazine, helped create the mythical town of Hannibal, home of boyhood at its most idyllic and innocent, that Americans still cherish today as the childhood home of their beloved Mark Twain.*

Beautiful for situation is the lovely little city of Hannibal, on the Mississippi, the boyhood home of Mr. Samuel L. Clemens, known the world over as "Mark Twain." The hills are high, the valley is picturesque, the houses are handsome and comfortable. The town claims a population of fifteen thousand, and is just now enjoying a boom, recent discoveries of deposits having been made that will greatly enrich the place. On a late visit I endeavored to gather some information regarding Hannibal's "first citizen," with the following result. . . .

The local tradition remembers the father of the humorist, "Squire" Clemens, as a good and peaceable citizen. He brought to the town with him his wife and children, and nothing unusual is remembered of the family, except that Mrs. Clemens had a peculiar and interesting drawl in her speech. When her son lectured in the town theater she called the attention of the neighbors to the fact that "Sam had a mighty long drawl to his talk, and she wondered where in the world he got it." Whereupon an old farmer remarked: "If the dam is a pacer, you will very likely find an amble in the colt." They brought up their children as well as circumstances would allow, considering three things, the Civil War, the West on the river, and the children. It is generally believed that Aunt Polly in "Tom Sawyer" was "Sam's" own mother, and that Tom was Sam. If this is so, one can almost read the family history in that captivating little book.

"Oh, yes, I knowed Sam," recently said an old resident whose name had been given to me as one of the few still living who had something to say of the youth of the writer. "I knowed him when he was a boy. He was a printer's devil,—I think that's what they called him,—and they didn't miss it: he surely had lots of mischief in him. We boys used to go of a Sunday down to the cave and git into all kinds of rascality. Sam was very good on a joke. Last I saw of him round here was when he went to the war."

A favorite sport of the boys was to go to a high hill near an old mill, and start a loose rock down the steep side until, gathering force and velocity, it finally went crashing into the water below. On one occasion an ill-directed missile assailed the mill and made a hole through it like the path of a thirty-pounder. The miller ran out and lifted up his voice in prayer, beseeching Heaven to spare him and his property, promising, if the prayer was answered, never to ask another favor of the Almighty while he lived. One immense boulder, partly buried in

It was here in Hannibal that Sam was to have his first experience in school. When he was four and a half he was sent to a dame school kept by Elizabeth Horr, the cooper's wife, in a small log house at the end of South Main Street. The terms were twenty-five cents a week. Piety, good manners, reading, recitation, long division, and spelling were the subjects taught, through third grade. . . .

It was desperation that dictated sending Sam to school, for he was a "backward," uncommunicative child, the least promising of the lot. He was still hyperactive, and if not watched every minute, would run away—invariably toward the river. Whenever that happened, Jane Lampton expected momentarily to have someone bring him home half dead. With Henry now a toddler, Sam was more than she could handle. Further, she hoped that learning might draw him out, and that discipline would curb his antics.

Rules were many and strict at school. Sam never forgot his first day because he broke a rule without knowing it and was warned that a second breach would bring a whipping. Presently, he repeated the offense and Mrs. Horr sent him outside to get a switch. In the mud not far from the door he found a cooper's shaving two inches wide and a quarter-inch thick, old and rotting. He brought it in, placed it on her desk, and waited with an attitude of meekness and resignation which he believed would win her sympathy—the head, crowned with a "dense ruck" of short, auburn curls just like his mother's, slightly bowed, the blue-grey eyes (which sometimes looked green) cast down. Instead, after a few seconds of oppressive silence, she addressed him by his full name—it was the first time he had ever heard Samuel Langhorne Clemens strung together "in one procession"—said she was ashamed of him, and sent an older boy to cut a proper switch. The lesson learned was that when a teacher calls a boy by his entire name, trouble is in store.

from MARK TWAIN: THE BACHELOR YEARS, *by Margaret Sanborn*

1848

John A. Sutter discovers gold at his mill on the American River near Sacramento, California. The gold rush that follows eventually sends thousands to northern California. In 1850 alone, more than forty-two thousand seekers of gold make their way west, many passing through MT's hometown of Hannibal, Missouri.

1848

Lucretia Mott and Elizabeth Cady Stanton stage a women's convention at Seneca Falls, New York, to discuss women's rights, specifically the right to vote and the right to control property.

1849

Henry David Thoreau publishes "Civil Disobedience," an essay that grew out of his arrest and incarceration after refusing to pay a poll tax.

the hillside, promised to the mind of young Sam a lot of fun. He called the boys together and thus addressed them: "Fellows, this is a bigger rock than ever rolled down any hill; it will take lots of work to move her, but when she starts, all the world can't stop her. We can lift her out, I will be the boss, and you fellows work, and we will see the greatest thing that ever happened." Many Sundays were spent in toiling at the sides and underneath the great rock. The "boss" never for one moment lost his nerve, but cheered the others on in their work, until one day they succeeded in turning over the great mass of stone. Over and over it went, and faster and faster, till the boys were frightened and almost out of their senses. They did not know where or how the thing would stop. It was making for the road which wound around the hill; some one might be passing; or, even if not, the way might be forever blockaded. They watched and wondered. At last it struck the road with tremendous power, and taking a mighty leap, landed in the channel of the Mississippi River. Of course, no one knew who did it. . . .

In his writings, Mr. Clemens sometimes gives the real name of one of his characters, and one will find, upon investigation, that his picture is true to life. Among these, I will mention two extremes, Huckleberry Finn and Laura Hawkins, who figures as Becky Thatcher. One was in the lower walks of life, living on charity, sleeping in old barrels, and covering himself with such rags as might fall to his lot; the other was a beautiful, accomplished girl, a strong and

Located 150 miles above St. Louis on the Mississippi River in the northeastern corner of Missouri, Hannibal was home to Samuel Clemens from 1839 to 1853. When the Clemens family arrived, the town consisted of only a handful of brick houses among a larger number of older log cabins. All around was forest and open prairie and a scattering of farms. But it was not long before Hannibal enjoyed a burst of growth. Situated in a valley carved by the waters of Bear Creek as it made its way to the Mississippi, Hannibal came alive during the 1840s and '50s. The hundreds of steamboats that traveled up and down the great river every day found a convenient and easy landing point in Hannibal; and for travelers on land, the city marked the end of the East and the beginning of the West—the perfect place for one last pause before entering the unknown frontier. Hannibal had sawmills, tobacco factories, slaughterhouses, saloons, bookdealers, newspapers; and, thanks to the constant traffic of steamboats, it had pioneers, prospectors, actors, gamblers, lecturers, circus performers, and a mix of people to be found in few other places in America. Of the daily arrival of the steamboats, Clemens later wrote, "Before these events, the day was glorious with expectancy; after them, the day was a dead and empty thing." At right, Clemens outside his Hannibal home in 1902. Photo The Mark Twain House.

lovely character, the pride and belle of the village. It was lately my good fortune to meet the lady, Mrs. F——, whose youth was thus celebrated. . . .

"Sam was always up to some mischief," said "Becky" to me. "We attended Sunday School together, and they had a system of rewards for saying verses after committing them to memory. A blue ticket was given for ten verses, a red ticket for ten blue, a yellow for ten red, and a Bible for ten yellow tickets. If you count that up, you will see it makes a Bible for ten thousand verses. Sam came up one Sunday with his ten yellow tickets, and everybody knew he hadn't said a verse, but had just got them by trading with the boys. But he received his Bible with all the serious air of a diligent student. He took me out when I was first learning to skate, and I fell on the ice with such force as to make me unconscious; but he did not forsake me. We had many happy experiences." . . .

Mr. Clemens holds a safe place in the affections and esteem of the citizens of Hannibal. His name is a household word, a possession of local pride, and all claim a personal interest in their gifted fellow-citizen. How wonderful is the spell of humor! As long as boys shall climb those hills or float along the Mississippi, as long indeed as the English language is read, the name of "Mark Twain" will be known and honored, and the mere mention of the humorist will serve to bring a smile to the face of sorrow and lighten the burdens of many a weary life.

BOYHOOD'S END

FROM *THE AUTOBIOGRAPHY OF MARK TWAIN*, EDITED BY CHARLES NEIDER

In this section from his autobiography—Charles Neider's version of it—Clemens begins telling about his father's death but manages to end with a humorous recounting of one of his favorite pranks from his apprentice days in the Hannibal shop of the printer Joseph Ament. The story is testament to Clemens's unique style of autobiography, as well as proof that from a very early age he was thrilled by the power of the printed word to amuse and incite.

When my father died, in 1847, the disaster happened—as is the customary way with such things—just at the very moment when our fortunes had changed and we were about to be comfortable once more after several years of grinding poverty and privation which had been inflicted upon us by the dishonest act of one Ira Stout, to whom my father had lent several thousand dollars—a fortune in those days and in that region. My father had just been elected clerk of the Surrogate Court. This modest prosperity was not only quite sufficient for us and for our ambitions, but he was so esteemed—held in such high regard and honor throughout the county—that his occupancy of that dignified office would, in the opinion of everybody, be his possession as long as he might live. He went to Palmyra, the county-seat, to be sworn in about the end of February. In returning home horseback twelve miles a storm of sleet and rain assailed him and he arrived at the house in a half-frozen condition. Pleurisy followed and he died on the 24th of March.

Thus our splendid new fortune was snatched from us and we were in the depths of poverty again. It is the way such things are accustomed to happen. The Clemens family was penniless again.

Orion did not come to Hannibal until two or three years after my father's death. He remained in St. Louis. He was a journeyman printer and earning wages. Out of his wage he supported my mother and my brother Henry, who was two years younger than I. My sister Pamela helped in this support by taking piano pupils. Thus we got along, but it was pretty hard sledding. I was not one of the burdens, because I was taken from school at once upon my father's death and placed in the office of the Hannibal *Courier* as printer's apprentice, and Mr. Ament, the editor and proprietor of the paper, allowed me the usual emolument of the office of apprentice—that is to say, board and clothes but no money. The clothes consisted of two suits a year but one of the suits always failed to materialize and the other suit was not purchased so long as Mr. Ament's old clothes held out. I was only about half as big as Ament, consequently his shirts gave me the uncomfortable sense of living in a circus tent, and I had to turn up his pants to my ears to make them short enough.

There were two other apprentices. One was Wales McCormick, seventeen or eighteen years old and a giant. When he was in Ament's clothes they fitted him like the candle mold fits the candle—thus he was generally in a suffocated condition, particularly in the summertime. He was a reckless, hilarious, admirable creature; he had no principles and was delightful company. At first we three apprentices had to feed in the kitchen with the old slave cook and her very handsome and bright and well-behaved young mulatto daughter. . . .

We got but little variety in the way of food at that kitchen table and there wasn't enough of it anyway. So we apprentices used to keep alive by arts of our own—that is to say, we crept into the cellar nearly every night by a private entrance which we had discovered and we robbed the cellar of potatoes and onions and such things and carried them downtown to the printing-office, where we slept on pallets on the floor and cooked them at the stove and had very good times. . . .

Once the celebrated founder of the at that time new and widespread sect called Campbellites arrived in our village from Kentucky and it made a prodigious excitement. The farmers and their families drove or tramped into the village from miles around to get a sight of the illustrious Alexander Campbell and to have a chance to hear him preach. When he preached in a church many had to be disappointed, for there was no church that would begin to hold all the applicants; so in order to accommodate all, he preached in the open air in the public square and that was the first time in my life that I had realized what a mighty population this planet contains when you get them all together.

He preached a sermon on one of these occasions which he had written especially for that occasion. All the Campbellites wanted it printed, so that they could save it and read it over and over again and get it by heart. So they drummed up sixteen dollars, which was a large sum then, and for this great sum Mr. Ament contracted to print five hundred copies of that sermon and put them in yellow paper covers. It was a sixteen-page duodecimo pamphlet and it was a great event in our office. As we regarded it, it was a book, and it promoted us to the dignity of book printers. Moreover, no such mass of actual money as sixteen dollars, in one bunch, had ever entered that office on any previous occasion. People didn't pay for their paper and for their advertising in money; they paid in dry-goods, sugar, coffee, hickory wood, oak wood, turnips, pumpkins, onions, watermelons—and it was very seldom indeed that a man paid in money, and when that happened we thought there was something the matter with him.

We set up the great book in pages—eight pages to a form—and by help of a printer's manual we managed to get the pages in their apparently crazy but really sane places on the imposing-stone. We printed that form on a Thursday. Then we set up the remaining eight pages, locked them into a form and struck a proof. Wales read the proof and presently was aghast, for he had struck a snag. And it was a bad time to strike a snag, because it was Saturday; it was approaching noon; Saturday afternoon was our holiday and we wanted to get away and go fishing. At such a time as this Wales struck that snag and showed us what had happened. He had left out a couple of words in a thin-spaced page of solid matter and there wasn't another break-line for two or three pages ahead. What in the world was to be done? Overrun all those pages to get in the two missing words? Apparently there was no other way. It would take an hour to do it. Then a revise must be sent to the great minister; we must wait for him to read the revise; if he encountered any errors we must correct them. It looked as if we might lose half the afternoon before we could get away.

Then Wales had one of his brilliant ideas. In the line in which the "out" had been made occurred the name Jesus Christ. Wales reduced it in the French way to J. C. It made room for the missing words but it took 99 percent of the solemnity out of a particularly solemn sentence. We sent off the revise and waited. We were not intending to wait long. In the circumstances we meant to get out and go fishing before that revise should get back, but we were not speedy enough. Presently that great Alexander Campbell appeared at the far end of that sixty-foot room, and his countenance cast a gloom over the whole place. He strode down to our end and what he said was brief, but it was very stern and it was to the point. He read Wales a lecture. He said, "So long as you live, don't you ever diminish the Saviour's name again. Put it *all* in." He repeated this admonition a couple of times to emphasize it, then he went away.

In that day the common swearers of the region had a way of their own of *emphasizing* the Saviour's name when they were using it profanely and this fact intruded itself into Wales's incorrigible mind. It offered him an opportunity for a momentary entertainment which seemed to him to be more precious and more valuable than even fishing and swimming could afford. So he imposed upon himself the long and weary and dreary task of overrunning all those three pages in order to improve upon his former work and incidentally and thoughtfully improve upon the great preacher's admonition. He enlarged the offending J. C. into Jesus H. Christ. Wales knew that that would make prodigious trouble and it did. But it was not in him to resist it. He had to succumb to the law of his make. I don't remember what his punishment was but he was not the person to care for that. He had already collected his dividend.

In his autobiography, Clemens states that he was removed from school to become an apprentice "at once upon his father's death"; but Joseph Ament, the printer to whom Clemens was engaged, did not arrive in Hannibal until 1848, more than a year after John Marshall Clemens had passed away. Clemens's revision gives the story of his apprenticeship a greater sense of urgency, but it does not overstate the importance of this turning point in Clemens's life. The apprenticeship marked the beginning of his independence, and it also provided his first, albeit precarious, connection to the world of the printed word. In Mr. Ament's shop, Clemens was introduced to the literature of the day, some of it badly written and poorly conceived, but enough of merit and interest to light a spark in the young boy's mind. That spark was further ignited by a book page Clemens claimed he found blowing in the wind on a Hannibal street. Torn from a book on the life of Joan of Arc, the page, Clemens recalled, opened his eyes to the powerful effect of good writing and did what school had never been able to do—made him an avid reader. Above, the earliest known photograph of Sam Clemens, taken in 1850. Photo The Mark Twain Papers.

Mark Twain

FROM PRINTER TO PILOT
1853–1861

Clemens was not quite eighteen years old when he left Hannibal in 1853. For the next four years, he supported himself as a journeyman printer in St. Louis, New York, Philadelphia, Iowa, and finally in Cincinnati, where his dreams outgrew the confines of the typesetting room and sent him down river on the Mississippi toward South America. He planned to find adventure and fortune as an explorer on the Amazon River, but the river of his youth reclaimed Clemens and put an end to his South American dreams. As a boy in Hannibal, Clemens had imagined piloting a Mississippi steamboat; en route to the Amazon, he revived that dream and apprenticed himself to Horace Bixby, the acclaimed pilot of the steamboat *PAUL JONES*. The great Mississippi, the river of his childhood, now became Sam Clemens's home and his university.

Illustration at right by Norman Rockwell from THE ADVENTURES OF TOM SAWYER, *1936 edition.*

LEAVING HANNIBAL

FROM *THE AUTOBIOGRAPHY OF MARK TWAIN*, EDITED BY CHARLES NEIDER

1853

MT leaves Hannibal in June at the age of seventeen.

1853–1857

MT supports himself as a journeyman printer in St. Louis, New York, Philadelphia, and Iowa.

1853

The Crystal Palace Exhibition of the Industry of All Nations opens in New York City; among its thousands of visitors is MT.

1854

The Kansas-Nebraska Act creates two new U.S. territories and allows for popular sovereignty on the issue of slavery. This contradicts the Missouri Compromise of 1820, which had declared that all new territory north of Missouri's southern border would be free. The act leads to violence in the territories and heats up tensions between abolitionist and pro-slavery factions throughout the nation.

1854

Henry David Thoreau publishes WALDEN.

1855

Walt Whitman publishes LEAVES OF GRASS, a book of twelve poems, at his own expense. The book, largely ignored in its day, will one day become one of the most popular books of poetry in American literature.

There is only one thing that gets my "dander" up—and that is the hands are always encouraging me: telling me "it's no use to get discouraged—no use to be down-hearted, for there is more work here than you can do!" "Downhearted," the devil! I have not had a particle of such a feeling since I left Hannibal, more than four months ago. I fancy they'll have to wait some time till they see me downhearted or afraid of starving while I have strength to work and am in a city of 400,000 inhabitants.

Samuel Clemens in Philadelphia, from a letter to Orion, October 26–28, 1853

Clemens left Hannibal in 1853. His immediate goal was New York City and the Crystal Palace Exhibition of All Nations. In this selection from his autobiography, Clemens tells how his trip to New York City led to three years on the road and a new direction for his life.

About 1849 or 1850 Orion severed his connection with the printing-house in St. Louis and came up to Hannibal and bought a weekly paper called the Hannibal *Journal*, together with its plant and its good-will, for the sum of five hundred dollars cash. He borrowed the cash at ten per cent interest from an old farmer named Johnson who lived five miles out of town. Then he reduced the subscription price of the paper from two dollars to one dollar. He reduced the rates for advertising in about the same proportion and thus he created one absolute and unassailable certainty—to wit: that the business would never pay him a single cent of profit.

He took me out of the *Courier* office and engaged my services in his own at three dollars and a half a week, which was an extravagant wage, but Orion was always generous, always liberal with everybody except himself. It cost him nothing in my case, for he was never able to pay me a single penny as long as I was with him. By the end of the first year he found he must make some economies. The office rent was cheap but it was not cheap enough. He could not afford to pay rent of any kind, so he moved the whole plant into the house we lived in, and it cramped the dwelling-place cruelly. He kept that paper alive during four years but I have at this time no idea how he accomplished it. Toward the end of each year he had to turn out and scrape and scratch for the fifty dollars of interest due Mr. Johnson, and that fifty dollars was about the only cash he ever received or paid out, I suppose, while he was proprietor of that newspaper, except for ink and printing-paper. The paper was a dead failure. It had to be that from the start.

Finally, he handed it over to Mr. Johnson and headed up to Muscatine, Iowa, and acquired a small interest in a weekly newspaper there. . . . He came across a winning and pretty girl who lived in Quincy, Illinois, a few miles below Keokuk, and they became engaged. He was always falling in love with girls but by some accident or other he had never gone so far as engagement before. And now he achieved nothing but misfortune by it, because he straightaway fell in love with a Keokuk girl—at least he imagined he was in love with her . . . and he was in a great quandary. He didn't know whether to marry the Keokuk one or the Quincy one, or whether to try to marry both of them and suit every one concerned. But the Keokuk girl soon settled that for him. She was a master spirit and she ordered him to write the Quincy girl and break off that match, which he did. . . .

To gain a living in Muscatine was plainly impossible, so Orion and his new wife went to Keokuk to live, for she wanted to be near her relatives. He bought a little bit of a job-printing plant—on credit, of course—and at once put prices down to where not even the apprentices could get a living out of it, and this sort of thing went on.

I had not joined the Muscatine migration. Just before that happened . . . I disappeared one night and fled to St. Louis. There I worked in the composing-room of the *Evening News* for a time and then started on my travels to see the world. The world was New York City and there was a little World's Fair there. It had just been opened where the great reservoir afterward was and where the sumptuous public library is now being built—Fifth Avenue and 42nd Street. I arrived in New York with two or three dollars in pocket change and a ten-dollar bank bill concealed in the lining of my coat. I got work at villainous wages in the establishment of John A. Gray & Green in Cliff Street and I found board in a sufficiently villainous mechanics' boarding-house in Duane Street. The firm paid my wages in wildcat money at its face value, and my week's wage merely sufficed to pay board and lodging. By and by I went to Philadelphia and worked there some months as a "sub" on the *Inquirer* and the *Public Ledger*. Finally I made a flying trip to Washington to see the sights there, and in 1854 I went back to the Mississippi Valley, sitting upright in the smoking-car two or three days and nights. When I reached St. Louis I was exhausted. I went to bed on board a steamboat that was bound for Muscatine. I fell asleep at once, with my clothes on, and didn't wake again for thirty-six hours.

I worked in that little job office in Keokuk as much as two years, I should say, without ever collecting a cent of wages, for Orion was never able to pay anything—but Dick Higham and I had good times. I don't know what Dick got, but it was probably only uncashable promises.

One day in the midwinter of 1856 or 1857—I think it was 1856—I was coming along the main street of Keokuk in the middle of the forenoon. It was bitter weather—so bitter that that street was deserted, almost. A light dry snow was blowing here and there on the ground and on the pavement, swirling this way and that way and making all sorts of beautiful figures, but very chilly to look at. The wind blew a piece of paper past me and it lodged against a wall of a house. Something about the look of it attracted my attention and I gathered it in. It was a fifty-dollar bill, the only one I had ever seen, and the largest assemblage of money I had ever seen in one spot. I advertised it in the papers and suffered more than a thousand dollars' worth of solicitude and fear and distress during the next few days lest the owner should see the advertisement and come and take my fortune away. As many as four days went by without an applicant; then I could endure this kind of misery no longer. I felt sure that another four could not go by in this safe and secure way. I felt that I must take that money out of danger. So I bought a ticket for Cincinnati and went to that city.

Working for his brother's newspaper brought Sam no financial reward, but did provide insight into his future. Orion encouraged his brother to write humorous sketches, news stories, and poetry. When business called Orion out of town for a week, he handed the editorial reigns over to Sam—with unforgettable results. Sam took his responsibility to heart, and set about filling the paper with the most provocative, libelous, and humorous material he could produce. He lampooned a fellow editor, criticized the paper's own poet, and took shots at more than one of Hannibal's prominent residents. The result was a barrage of criticism, and also a surge in subscriptions. Sam may not have pleased his brother, but he was not soon to forget the exhilarating feeling of power his brief reign had provided.

New York is at present overstocked with printers; and I suppose they are from the South, driven North by the yellow fever. I got a permanent situation on Monday morning, in a book and job office, and went to work. The printers here are badly organized, and therefore have to work for various prices. These prices are 23, 25, 28, 30, 32, and 35 cents per 1,000 ems. The price I get is 23 cents; but I did very well to get a place at all, for there are thirty or forty—yes, fifty good printers in the city with no work at all; besides, my situation is permanent, and I shall keep it till I can get a better one. The office I work in is John A. Gray's, 97 Cliff Street, and, next to Harper's, is the most extensive in the city. In the room in which I work I have forty compositors for company. Taking compositors, pressmen, stereotypers, and all, there are about two hundred persons employed in the concern. The "Knickerbocker," "New York Recorder," "Choral Advocate," "Jewish Chronicle," "Littell's Living Age," "Irish—," and half a dozen other papers and periodicals are printed here, besides an immense number of books. They are very particular about spacing, justification, proofs, etc., and even if I do not make much money, I will learn a great deal. I thought Ustick was particular enough, but acknowledge now that he was not old-maidish. Why, you must put exactly the same space between every two words, and every line must be spaced alike. They think it dreadful to space one line with three em spaces, and the next one with five ems. However, I expected this, and worked accordingly from the beginning; and out of all the proofs I saw, without boasting, I can say mine was by far the cleanest. In St. Louis, Mr. Baird said my proofs were the cleanest that were ever set in his office. The foreman of the Anzeiger told me the same—foreman of the Watchman the same; and with all this evidence, I believe I do set a clean proof. . . .

In going to and from my meals, I go by the way of Broadway—and to cross Broadway is the rub—but once across, it is the rub for two or three squares. My plan—and how could I choose another, when there is no other—is to get into the crowd; and when I get in, I am borne, and rubbed, and crowded along, and need scarcely trouble myself about using my own legs; and when I get out, it seems like I had been pulled to pieces and very badly put together. . . .

Samuel Clemens, from a letter to Jane Lampton Clemens, August 31, 1853

PERPLEXING LESSONS

FROM *LIFE ON THE MISSISSIPPI*, BY MARK TWAIN

1856

MT moves to Cincinnati in October.

1856

The first railroad bridge across the Mississippi River connects Rock Island, Illinois, and Davenport, Iowa.

1857

The Dred Scott decision by the United States Supreme Court declares that because slaves are not citizens, Scott, a slave in Missouri who was taken to Illinois—a free state—and then returned to Missouri, cannot sue for his freedom based upon his temporary residency in a free state. The Court further declares that the Missouri Compromise of 1820 is unconstitutional because the federal government has no authority to prohibit slavery in the territories.

1857

The ATLANTIC MONTHLY magazine begins publication in Boston. One of the magazine's leading contributors will be William Dean Howells, one of the first of the American literary establishment to recognize the talent of MT.

1857

MT decides to explore the Amazon and leaves Cincinnati for South America aboard the steamship PAUL JONES.

1857

MT becomes cub pilot on the steamboat PAUL JONES on the Mississippi River.

1858

A series of seven debates take place in Illinois between Senate candidates Stephen Douglas and the little-known Abraham Lincoln. The debates are symbolic of the conflict that threatens the security of the American Union. Douglas argues repeatedly that issues such as slavery are the domain of the states and territories. Lincoln, eloquently arguing that "a house divided against itself cannot stand," declares that the entire country must be slave or free if the Union is going to survive. Lincoln loses the election but gains national recognition.

In Cincinnati, Clemens hatched a scheme to strike it rich as an Amazon explorer, and he set out by steamboat to New Orleans, where he hoped to secure passage to South America. Finding no such passage available, he gave in to the lure of the river (not to mention the demands of his pocketbook) and convinced the captain of the PAUL JONES, *Horace Bixby, to take him on as a cub pilot. Bixby proved a thorough teacher, but Clemens was to learn even more from the river itself and from the life that thrived on its waters and along its banks. In this excerpt from* LIFE ON THE MISSISSIPPI, *he describes the difficulty of learning the ever-changing river.*

At the end of what seemed a tedious while, I had managed to pack my head full of islands, towns, bars, "points," and bends; and a curiously inanimate mass of lumber it was, too. However, inasmuch as I could shut my eyes and reel off a good long string of these names without leaving out more than ten miles of river in every fifty, I began to feel that I could take a boat down to New Orleans if I could make her skip those little gaps. But of course my complacency could hardly get start enough to lift my nose a trifle into the air, before Mr. Bixby would think of something to fetch it down again. One day he turned on me suddenly with this settler:

"What is the shape of Walnut Bend?"

He might as well have asked me my grandmother's opinion of protoplasm. I reflected respectfully, and then said I didn't know it had any particular shape. My gun-powdery chief went off with a bang, of course, and then went on loading and firing until he was out of adjectives.

I had learned long ago that he only carried just so many rounds of ammunition, and was sure to subside into a very placable and even remorseful old smooth-bore as soon as they were all gone. That word "old" is merely affectionate; he was not more than thirty-four. I waited. By and by he said:

"My boy, you've got to know the *shape* of the river perfectly. It is all there is left to steer by on a very dark night. Everything else is blotted out and gone. But mind you, it hasn't the same shape in the night that it has in the daytime."

"How on earth am I ever going to learn it, then?"

"How do you follow a hall at home in the dark? Because you know the shape of it. You can't see it."

"Do you mean to say that I've got to know all the million trifling variations of shape in the banks of this interminable river as well as I know the shape of the front hall at home?"

"On my honor, you've got to know them *better* than any man ever did know the shapes of the halls in his own house."

"I wish I was dead!"'

"Now, I don't want to discourage you, but—"

"Well, pile it on me; I might as well have it now as another time."

"You see, this has got to be learned; there isn't any getting around it. A clear starlight night throws such heavy shadows that, if you didn't know the shape of a shore perfectly, you would claw away from every bunch of timber, because you would take the black shadow of it for a solid cape; and you see you would be getting scared to death every fifteen minutes by the watch. You would be fifty yards from shore all the time when you ought to be within fifty feet of it. You can't see a snag in one of those shadows, but you know exactly where it is, and the shape of the river tells you when you are coming to it. Then there's your pitch-dark night; the river is a very different shape on a pitch-dark night from what it is on a star-light night. All shores seem to be straight lines, then, and mighty dim ones, too; and you'd *run* them for straight lines, only you know better. You boldly drive your boat right into what seems to be a solid, straight wall (you knowing very well that in reality there is a curve there), and that wall falls back and makes way for you. Then there's your gray mist. You take a night when there's one of these grisly, drizzly, gray mists, and then there isn't *any* particular shape to a shore. A gray mist would tangle the head of the oldest man that ever lived. Well, then, different kinds of *moonlight* change the shape of the river in different ways. You see—"

"Oh, don't say any more, please! Have I got to learn the shape of the river according to all these five hundred thousand different ways? If I tried to carry all that cargo in my head it would make me stoop-shouldered."

"*No!* you only learn *the* shape of the river; and you learn it with such absolute certainty that you can always steer by the shape that's *in your head,* and never mind the one that's before your eyes."

"Very well, I'll try it; but, after I have learned it, can I depend on it? Will it keep the same form and not go fooling around?"

Before Mr. Bixby could answer, Mr. W. came in to take the watch, and he said:

"Bixby, you'll have to look out for President's Island, and all that country clear away up above the Old Hen and Chickens. The banks are caving and the shape of the shores changing like everything. Why, you wouldn't know the point above 40. You can go up inside the old sycamore snag, now."

So that question was answered. Here were leagues of shore changing shape. My spirits were down in the mud again. Two things seemed pretty apparent to me. One was, that in order to be a pilot a man had got to learn more than any one man ought to be allowed to know; and the other was, that he must learn it all over again in a different way every twenty-four hours.

Clemens received his pilot's license on April 9, 1859. His career lasted for two years, until, in April of 1861, it was grounded by the Civil War. Years later, Clemens wrote: "[Whenever I come upon a] well-drawn character in fiction or biography, I generally take a warm personal interest in him, for the reason that I have known him before—met him on the river." Above, Clemens during his piloting years. Photo The Mark Twain House.

The term steamboat refers to a steam-powered vessel built to travel inland waterways. Steamboats became part of American life in the early years of the nineteenth century, and by 1811 they were carrying passengers and cargo up and down the great Mississippi River, creating a revolution in commerce and a whole new subculture of American life. Sam Clemens and his family lived in Hannibal during the town's heyday as a steamboat port. In the 1830s, there were two hundred steamboats on the Mississippi. This number tripled during the next two decades, and by the time Clemens himself had become a pilot there were close to one thousand boats working the great waterway, making steamboat pilots among the most highly esteemed members of Mississippi River society. The steamboat era had ended by the time Clemens began writing novels under the name Mark Twain, but his romantic and vivid descriptions of life along the Mississippi River fixed the steamboat forever in the American imagination. At left, a nineteenth century Mississippi River steamboat. Photo The Mark Twain House.

A BRIEF, SHARP SCHOOLING

FROM MARK TWAIN: THE BACHELOR YEARS, BY MARGARET SANBORN

1858

The steamship PENNSYLVANIA explodes on the Mississippi River near Memphis, Tennessee, killing 160 people, including MT's younger brother Henry, who was working aboard the steamship at the time of the accident. MT, who secured the job for Henry aboard the PENNSYLVANIA, blames himself for his brother's death.

1858

Overland mail service connecting the East and West coasts of the United States is inaugurated.

1858

Gold is discovered near Pike's Peak, Colorado, sending thousands of hopeful prospectors to the West.

1859

The radical abolitionist John Brown leads a raid on a federal arsenal at Harper's Ferry in what is now West Virginia. Brown plans to use the weapons to arm an army of fugitive slaves and abolitionists in order to fight slavery in the Appalachian region. Brown is captured and later hanged for murder and treason by the state of Virginia. In the South, Brown is reviled as a traitor to his country and a murderer; in the North, thanks in great part to public support by writers Henry David Thoreau and Henry Wadsworth Longfellow, he is considered a martyr for the cause of freedom.

1859

MT is granted his license to pilot steamboats on the Mississippi River on April 9.

1860

Republican candidate Abraham Lincoln is elected president of the United States in November elections.

1860

South Carolina becomes the first American state to secede from the Union, a move made in protest to the election of Abraham Lincoln to the presidency.

Clemens gathered an immeasurable amount of fact and legend from his days as a riverboat pilot, which he preserved and would later transform into works of fiction. In the eyes of biographer Margaret Sanborn, the Mississippi River was Clemens's university.

At last there came a day when Sam felt confident enough to be examined by the Inspectors of the District of St. Louis. On April 9, 1859, he was passed by them and granted a pilot's certificate licensing him to navigate the Mississippi River between St. Louis and New Orleans for one year, when he would have to be re-examined. He then began earning $250 a month, a "princely salary," his first pay since April 1857, when he had started his apprenticeship. Shortly, he could count on banking one hundred of it regularly, as well as send money to his mother and Orion. By the end of 1860, he was able to speculate in the New Orleans produce market for his own and Orion's benefit, and in letters to him quoted current prices for chickens, eggs, and apples, and their fluctuations. He had invested in 3,600 dozen eggs at fifteen cents a dozen, and now they were down to twelve and a half cents; and 18 barrels of apples for which he had expected to get six or seven dollars a barrel, and now, "not worth a d–mn." But he had stored the "infernal" produce and would wait for prices to rise. . . .

Not long after getting his license, Sam was assigned to the *City of Memphis*, which, he was pleased to tell his family, "is the largest boat in the trade and the hardest to pilot, *and* consequently I can get a reputation on her, which is a thing I never could accomplish on a

Three of Clemens's major novels deal extensively with steamboats. THE GILDED AGE features an extensive account of westward travel aboard a riverboat. ADVENTURES OF HUCKLEBERRY FINN highlights both the beauty and the danger of these great vessels as Huck and Jim navigate their raft through the heavy steamboat traffic. And PUDDN'HEAD WILSON takes place in the Mississippi River town of Dawson's Landing, where steamboats are a prominent part of everyday life. PUDDN'HEAD's Roxy seems to speak for the author who created her when she says, "If there was anything better in this world than steamboating, it was the glory to be got by telling about it." At right, Clemens during his piloting days. Photo The Mark Twain House.

transient boat." He is "also lucky in having a berth, while all other young pilots are idle. . . . Bless me! what a pleasure there is in revenge!—and what vast respect Prosperity commands! Why, six months ago, I could enter the Rooms [Pilot Association rooms] and receive only a nod, but now they say, 'Why how *are* you, old fellow—when did you get in?' And the young pilots who used to tell me patronizingly that I could never learn the river, cannot keep from showing a little of their chagrin at seeing me so far ahead of them. Permit me to 'blow my horn,' for I derive a living pleasure from these things, and when I go to pay my dues, I rather like to let the d---d rascals get a glimpse of a hundred dollar bill peeping out amongst notes of smaller dimensions, whose faces I do not exhibit! You will despise this egotism, but I tell you there is a 'stern joy in it.'" . . .

Clemens was aware that an entire world was compacted on and along the Mississippi River, and now he had the opportunity to become "personally and familiarly acquainted" with nearly every type of person to be met in life. As a boy he had noted the differences and peculiarities of children and adults, white and black, who lived in Hannibal, in the village of Florida, and on his uncle's farm. He had been interested in listening to their talk, their stories, jokes, songs, and music, and had retained much of it. On the river, he added immeasurably to that fund when he overheard the off-duty pilots gathered in the wheel-house talk about wrecks, fires, storms, and steamboat races; about river pirates and smugglers, and about John Murrell's gang, which had preyed upon rich travelers who went by land up and down the Mississippi. Between watches, he listened to the argot of professional gamblers, confidence men, and prostitutes from New Orleans and Natchez-under-the-Hill, who regularly took passage in order to ply their trades. In the cabin and on deck, he fell into conversation with wealthy cane and cotton planters and their families, with lawyers, land speculators, actors, itinerant portrait painters and tutors; with fortunetellers, politicians, preachers, and explorers; and with English, French, and German nobility touring the American West. They all, at some time, traveled up and down the river.

From native Southerners, most of them born story-tellers, he heard accounts of young women who passed as men, of premature burials, and cases of mistaken identity which had dire consequences. He heard about local feuds, murders for vengeance, and lynchings. Clemens called on much of this material in his writings, although not everything he used was published.

There were also the people with whom he had contact ashore at those points where the steamboats put in—woodyards, plantation landings, and "one-horse towns." Everywhere, he listened to the fine distinctions among regional dialects and became so adept he was able to use in his works the "Missouri negro dialect; the extremest form of the backwoods South Western dialect; the ordinary 'Pike County' dialect; and four modified varieties of the last," as he explained in a prefatory statement to *Adventures of Huckleberry Finn.* The shadings of these dialects were not done haphazardly, or by "guess-work, but painstakingly, and with the trustworthy guidance and support of personal familiarity with these several forms of speech."

Looking back much later, he realized that his profits from this "brief, sharp schooling" were many and various, and that to have obtained such an education ashore in "average" employment would have required as much as forty years. He came to think of the river as his university. It was certainly the perfect school for the writer of fiction.

Clemens, by all reports, was a skilled pilot who found consistent work on the river after earning his license. In ROUGHING IT, he recalled how his days as a pilot seemed very appealing during his vagabond years in the West. "I was a good average St. Louis and New Orleans pilot," he wrote, "and by no means ashamed of my abilities in that line; wages were two hundred and fifty dollars a month and no board to pay, and I did long to stand behind a wheel again and never roam anymore." Above, this painting by an unknown artist depicts Mark Twain aboard a steamboat. The painting now hangs in the Captiol Building, Jefferson City, Missouri. Photo SuperStock.

Mark Twain

THE BIRTH OF MARK TWAIN
1861-1867

The Civil War brought commerce on the Mississippi River to a halt and thus put an end to Sam Clemens's budding career as a steamboat pilot. Like most Missourians, Clemens had confused allegiances in the opening days of the Civil War. His home state had a distinctly Southern character and legal slavery. While the governor was calling for volunteers to join the Southern Rebellion, the state legislature voted not to join the Confederacy and Missouri remained officially loyal to the Union. Clemens joined a Confederate regiment, but proved an unenthusiastic Rebel; and when his unit disbanded after only two weeks, he gave up military life for good. In need of direction, Clemens looked west. In 1861, he left Missouri once again, this time for Nevada. Seeing the frontier was the fulfillment of a childhood dream, just as piloting on the Mississippi had been. But in the West, Clemens would discover more than the adventure and freedom he had imagined as a boy; he would discover his gift for writing. In Nevada and California in the 1860s, Sam Clemens became the writer Mark Twain.

Illustration at right by Norman Rockwell from THE ADVENTURES OF TOM SAWYER, *1936 edition*

FROM "THE PRIVATE HISTORY OF A CAMPAIGN THAT FAILED"

BY MARK TWAIN

1861

The Confederate States of America is formed at Montgomery, Alabama, on February 4. Member states are South Carolina, Mississippi, Florida, Alabama, Georgia, and Louisiana. Jefferson Davis is elected president of the Confederacy. Texas, Virginia, Arkansas, North Carolina, and Tennessee will later join the Confederate cause.

1861

Nevada and Dakota Territories are organized by a Congressional act on March 2.

1861

The American Civil War officially begins on April 12 in the harbor of Charleston, South Carolina, when Confederate troops on shore fire on the federal arsenal at Fort Sumter.

1861

Commerce on the Mississippi River is halted by the Civil War.

1861

Union troops move into Missouri under declaration of martial law.

In the earliest summer days of the war, I slipped out of Hannibal, Missouri, by night, with a friend, and joined a detachment of the rebel General Tom Harris' . . . army up a gorge behind an old barn in Ralls County. Colonel Ralls, of Mexican War celebrity, swore us in. He made us swear to uphold the flag and Constitution, . . . and to destroy every other military organization that we caught doing the same thing, which, being interpreted, means we were to repel invasion. Well, you see, this mixed us. We couldn't really tell which side we were on, but we went into camp and left it to the God of Battles. For that was the term then. I was made Second Lieutenant and Chief Mogul of a company of eleven men, who knew nothing about war— nor anything, for we had no captain. . . . We had a good enough time there at that barn, barring the rats

Clemens loved the life of a steamboat pilot—it was a life ever-changing, full of colorful characters, and not without a fair amount of prestige in the community. When the Civil War interrupted his happy life on the river, Clemens became an unenthusiastic soldier and remained devoted to the Rebel cause for only two weeks. Clemens was always somewhat uncomfortable talking about his actions during the war. When he did, it was under cover of humor.

You have heard from a great many people who did something in the war; is it not fair and right that you listen a little moment to one who started out to do something in it, but didn't? Thousands entered the war, got just a taste of it, and then stepped out again, permanently. These, by their very numbers, are respectable, and are therefore entitled to a sort of voice,—not a loud one, but a modest one; not a boastful one, but an apologetic one. They ought not to be allowed much space among better people—people who did something—I grant that; but they ought at least to be allowed to state why they didn't do anything, and also to explain the process by which they didn't do anything. Surely this kind of light must have a sort of value.

Out West there was a good deal of confusion in men's minds during the first months of the great trouble—a good deal of unsettledness, of leaning first this way, then that, then the other way. It was hard for us to get our bearings. I call to mind an instance of this. I was piloting on the Mississippi when the news came that South Carolina had gone out of the Union on the 20th of December, 1860. My pilot-mate was a New Yorker. He was strong for the Union; so was I. But he would not listen to me with any patience; my loyalty was smirched, to his eye, because my father had owned slaves. I said, in palliation of this dark fact, that I had heard my father say, some years before he died, that slavery was a great wrong, and that he would free the solitary negro he then owned if he could think it right to give away the property of the family when he was so straitened in means. My mate retorted that a mere impulse was nothing—anybody could pretend to a good impulse; and went on decrying my Unionism and libeling my ancestry. A month later the secession atmosphere had considerably thickened on the Lower Mississippi, and I became a rebel; so did he. We were together in New Orleans, the 26th of January, when Louisiana went out of the Union. He did his full share of the rebel shouting, but was bitterly opposed to letting me do mine. He said that I came of bad stock—of a father who had been willing to set slaves free. In the following summer he was piloting a Federal gunboat and shouting for the Union again, and I was in the Confederate army. I held his note for some borrowed money. He was one of the most upright men I ever knew; but he repudiated that note without hesitation, because I was a rebel, and the son of a man who owned slaves. . . .

The thoughtful will not throw this war-paper of mine lightly aside as being valueless. It has this value: it is a not unfair picture of what went on in many and many a militia camp in the first months of the rebellion, when the green recruits were without discipline, without the steadying and heartening influence of trained leaders; when all their circumstances were new and strange, and charged with exaggerated terrors, and before the invaluable experience of actual collision in the field had turned them from rabbits into soldiers. If this side of the picture of that early day has not before been put into history, then history has been to that degree incomplete, for it had and has its rightful place there. There was more Bull Run material scattered through the early camps of this country than exhibited itself at Bull Run. And yet it learned its trade presently, and helped to fight the great battles later. I could have become a soldier myself, if I had waited. I had got part of it learned; I knew more about retreating than the man that invented retreating.

Clemens spoke very little of his experiences in the Civil War, likely because those experiences were so brief and so conflicted. But the Civil War created the America in which Clemens could become Mark Twain, an America newly aware of the vast regional differences within its own culture, and, in many quarters, nostalgic for a way of life destroyed by the violent War Between the States. The Civil War brought on the legal end of slavery and preserved in name the union between North and South, but the nation was to remain long conflicted and divided. It was in that troubled post–war America that Mark Twain came to life and found an audience in every corner of the country. Above, an unknown artist paints Tom Sawyer at the river, one of countless images of the idyllic days of childhood inspired by the writing of Mark Twain. Photo SuperStock.

and the mosquitoes and the rain. We levied on both parties impartially, and both parties hated us impartially. But one day we heard that the invader was approaching, so we had to pack up and move, of course, and within twenty-four hours he was coming again. So we moved again. Next day he was after us once more. Well, we didn't like it much, but we moved, rather than make trouble. This went on for a week or ten days or more, and we saw considerable scenery.

There was mutiny and dissatisfaction all around, and of course, here came the enemy pestering us again—as much as two hours before breakfast, too, when nobody wanted to turn out, of course. This was a little too much. The whole command felt insulted. I detached one of my aides and sent him to the brigadier, and asked him to assign us to a district where there wasn't so much bother going on. The history of our campaign was laid before him, but instead of being touched by it, what did he do? He sent back an indignant message and said: "You have had a dozen chances inside of two weeks to capture the enemy, and he is still at large. (Well, we knew that!) Stay where you are this time, or I will court martial and hang the whole lot of you." Well, I submitted this brutal message to my battalion, and asked their advice. Said the orderly Sergeant: "If Tom Harris wants the enemy, let him come and get him. I ain't got any use for my share, and who's Tom Harris anyway, I'd like to know, that's putting on so many frills? Why, I knew him when he wasn't nothing but a darn telegraph operator. Gentlemen, you can do as you choose, as for me, I've got enough of this sashaying around so's you can't get a chance to pray, cause the time's all required for cussing, so off goes my war paint. You hear me!" The whole regiment said, with one voice, "That's the talk for me!" So there and then, on the spot, my brigade disbanded itself and tramped off home, with me at the tail of it. I hung up my own sword and returned to the arts of peace, and there were people who said I hadn't been absent from them yet. . . .

Samuel Clemens, from a Speech to the Boston Ancient and Honorable Artillery Company, October 1877

HEADING WEST

FROM *ROUGHING IT*, BY MARK TWAIN

1861

MT joins the Confederate cause as part of the Marion Rangers. The unit disbands after only two weeks, without ever having engaged with the enemy.

1861

MT and brother Orion leave St. Joseph, Missouri, by stagecoach in July and head for Nevada Territory.

1862

President Abraham Lincoln signs the Homestead Act to encourage settlement of the West. The act promises 160 acres of public land to any head of a household over the age of twenty-one who settles and remains on the land for five years. Eventually, two million settlers take advantage of Lincoln's offer.

1862

Jefferson Davis is inaugurated president of the Confederate States of America.

1862

MT settles in Virginia City, Nevada.

1862

MT is hired by the Virginia City TERRITORIAL ENTERPRISE as a reporter with the responsibility of covering the Nevada legislature.

1862

In April, the Battle of Shiloh pits Union forces under General Ulysses S. Grant against Confederate soldiers under the command of General Albert Johnston. The battle involves more than one hundred thousand men and results in severe losses on both sides. Public awareness of the tragedy of the Civil War is heightened by this bloody battle.

1862

President Lincoln signs a bill incorporating the Union Pacific Company, which plans to complete the first transcontinental railroad.

Conveniently for Clemens, the war that brought his piloting career to a halt had also affected life in the western territories. In the land that is now Nevada, recently discovered gold and silver became more important than ever to the Union with the demands of war. In March of 1861 the United States declared Nevada, which had been governed as part of Utah Territory for more than a decade, a distinct territory and rushed to set up a government. Orion Clemens, through a series of personal connections, won the job of secretary of the territory, second in rank only to the governor. He made plans to set out for Nevada immediately and asked his brother to join him in the unpaid capacity of secretary to the secretary. Sam readily agreed, excited mostly about the opportunities to strike it rich in the mineral-laden hills of the West. This passage from Mark Twain's 1872 novel ROUGHING IT *describes the mood of excitement and expectation as the Clemens brothers journeyed west.*

My brother had just been appointed Secretary of Nevada Territory—an office of such majesty that it concentrated in itself the duties and dignities of treasurer, comptroller, secretary of state, and acting governor in the governor's absence. A salary of eighteen hundred dollars a year and the title of "Mr. Secretary" gave to the great position an air of wild and imposing grandeur. I was young and ignorant, and I envied my brother. I coveted his distinction and his financial splendor, but particularly and especially the long, strange journey he was going to make, and the curious new world he was going to explore. He was going to travel! I never had been away from home, and that word "travel" had a seductive charm for me. Pretty soon he would be hundreds and hundreds of miles away on the great plains and deserts, and among the mountains of the Far West, and would see buffaloes and Indians, and prairie dogs, and antelopes, and have all kinds of adventures, and maybe get hanged or scalped, and have ever such a fine time, and write home and tell us all about it, and be a hero. And he would see the gold mines and the silver mines, and maybe go about of an afternoon when his work was done, and pick up two or three pailfuls of shining slugs, and nuggets of gold and silver on the hillside. And by and by he would become very rich, and return home by sea, and be able to talk as calmly about San Francisco and the ocean and "the isthmus" as if it was nothing of any consequence to have seen those marvels face to face. What I suffered in contemplating his happiness, pen cannot describe. And so, when he offered me, in cold blood, the sublime position of secretary under him, it appeared to me that the heavens and the earth passed away, and the firmament was rolled together as a scroll! I had nothing more to desire. My contentment was complete. At the end of an hour or two I was ready for the journey. Not much packing up was necessary, because we were going in the overland stage from the Missouri frontier to Nevada, and passengers were only allowed a small quantity of baggage apiece. There was no Pacific railroad in those fine times of ten or twelve years ago—not a single rail of it.

I only proposed to stay in Nevada three months—I had no thought of staying longer than that. I meant to see all I could that was new and strange, and then hurry home to business.

I little thought that I would not see the end of that three-month pleasure excursion for six or seven uncommonly long years!

I dreamed all night about Indians, deserts, and silver bars, and in due time, next day, we took shipping at the St. Louis wharf on board a steamboat bound up the Missouri River.

We were six days going from St. Louis to "St. Joe"—a trip that was so dull, and sleepy, and eventless that it has left no more impression on my memory than if its duration had been six minutes instead of that many days. No record is left in my mind, now, concerning it, but a confused jumble of savage-looking snags, which we deliberately walked over with one wheel or the other; and of reefs which we butted and butted, and then retired and climbed over in some softer place; and of sand bars which we roosted on occasionally, and rested, and then got out our crutches and sparred over. In fact, the boat might almost as well have gone to St. Joe by land, for she was walking most of the time, anyhow—climbing over reefs and clambering over snags patiently and laboriously all day long. The captain said she was a "bully" boat, and all she wanted was more "shear" and a bigger wheel. I thought she wanted a pair of stilts, but I had the deep sagacity not to say so.

Clemens found prospecting to be disappointing and fruitless, but in the West he did discover what was to be the true gold mine in his life—his talent for writing. Five years after he left the West, Clemens would publish his second novel, Roughing It, *based loosely and embroidered liberally upon his experiences in Nevada Territory. The work blends fact and fiction to create an engaging picture of the excitement and allure of the American frontier.* Roughing It *is of dubious value as a record of Clemens's life, but of immeasurable value as a depiction of life and times in the American West in the 1860s. Illustration from* Roughing It, *The Mark Twain House.*

Sam Clemens headed west with dreams of striking it rich, but like so many others he found the great wealth of gold and silver to be had in the American West frustratingly out of his reach. He staked several mining claims only to find out that claiming was the easy part, and that the actual mining was close to impossible without substantial funds and supplies. He then turned his attentions to timber, which was in demand to supply mine builders. Clemens and a friend staked a promising timber claim and then proceeded to burn it to the ground through the careless management of their campfire. Undaunted, Clemens stretched his planned three-month stay in the West into a visit of indefinite length. Illustration from Roughing It, *The Mark Twain House.*

THE TRUTH CONCERNING THIS LAND

SAMUEL CLEMENS, FROM A LETTER TO JANE LAMPTON CLEMENS, OCTOBER 26, 1861

1862

At the Battle of Antietam, General Robert E. Lee's first invasion of Northern territory is halted by General McClellan and his Union troops. Four thousand are killed and nearly twenty thousand are wounded.

1863

The Emancipation Proclamation is issued by President Lincoln.

1863

Edward Everett Hale publishes "The Man without a Country," a story inspired by the life of an anti-war Northerner who held President Lincoln responsible for the death and devastation of the Civil War and declared himself unwilling to live in a country governed by such a man. In Hale's story, the man is convicted of treason and sentenced to a life at sea, cut off from all news of his native land.

1863

The Battle of Gettysburg, fought in Pennsylvania in July, proves one of the most decisive and bloodiest battles of the Civil War. Combined, the two sides suffer more than fifty thousand casualties. In November, President Lincoln travels to Gettysburg to deliver the Gettysburg Address, three paragraphs that are considered among the most eloquent and noble words ever spoken by an American leader.

1863

MT visits San Francisco and begins occasional writing for the San Francisco MORNING CALL.

1863

MT adopts the pen name Mark Twain as his signature in newspaper writings.

1864

MT moves to San Francisco and begins to write regularly for the MORNING CALL.

1864

General Ulysses S. Grant takes command of Union troops.

This letter to his mother describing life in Nevada is perhaps one of Clemens's earliest attempts at travel writing, and it certainly hints at all the humor, irony, and exaggeration that will make his later, more formal attempts such a success.

You ask me in your last to tell you about the country—tell everything just as it is—no better and no worse—and *do* let nonsense alone. Very well, then, ma, since you wasted a considerable portion of your life in an unprofitable effort to teach me to tell the truth on all occasions, I will repay you by dealing strictly in facts just this once, and by avoiding that "nonsense" for which you seem to entertain a mild sort of horror. . . .

It never rains here, and the dew never falls. No flowers grow here, and no green thing gladdens the eye. The birds that fly over the land carry their provisions with them. Only the crow and the raven tarry with us. Our city lies in the midst of a desert of the purest, most unadulterated and uncompromising sand—in which infernal soil nothing but that fag-end of vegetable creation, "sage-brush," is mean enough to grow. If you will take a liliputian cedar tree for a model, and build a dozen imitations of it with the stiffest article of telegraph wire—set them one foot apart and then try to walk through them—you will understand, (provided the floor is covered twelve inches deep with sand) what it is to travel through a sage-brush desert. . . . As to the other fruits and flowers of the country, there ain't any except "Tula," a species of unpoetical rush, that grows on the banks of the Carson,—a RIVER, *ma mere,* twenty yards wide, knee-deep, and so villainously rapid and crooked, that it looks like it had wandered into the country without intending it, and had run about in a bewildered way and got lost in its hurry to get out again before some thirsty man came along and drank it up.

I said we are situated in a flat, sandy desert. True. And surrounded on all sides by such prodigious mountains that when you stand at a distance from Carson and gaze at them awhile,—until, by mentally measuring them, and comparing them with things of smaller size, you begin to conceive of their grandeur, and next to feel their vastness expanding your soul like a balloon, and ultimately find yourself growing, and swelling, and spreading into a colossus,—I say when this point is reached, you look disdainfully down upon the insignificant village of Carson, reposing like a cheap print away yonder at the foot of the big hills, and in that instant you are seized with a burning desire to stretch forth your hand, put the city in your pocket, and walk off with it. . . .

The houses are mostly frame, and unplastered; but "papered" inside with flour-sacks sewed together—with the addition, in favor of the parlor, of a second papering composed of engravings cut from "Harper's Weekly;" so you will easily perceive that the handsomer the "brand" upon the flour-sacks is, and the more spirited the pictures are, the finer the house looks. . . . On account of the dryness of the atmosphere, the shingles on the houses warp until they look very much like they would be glad to turn over, and lie awhile on the other side. . . .

Behold, I have spoken the truth concerning this land. And now, for your other questions, which shall be answered tersely, promptly, and to the point: First—"Do I go to church every Sunday?" Answer—"Scarsely [*sic*]." Second—"Have you a Church in Carson?" We have—a Catholic one—but, to use a fireman's expression, I believe "they don't run her now." We have also Protestant service nearly every Sabbath in the school house. Third—"Are there many ladies in Carson?" Multitudes—probably the handsomest in the world. Fourth—"Are the citizens generally moral and religious?" Prodigiously so. Fifth—"When my old friends ask me how you like Nevada, what reply shall I make?" Tell them I am *delighted* with it. It is the dustiest country on the face of the earth—but I rather like dust. And the days are very hot—but you know I am fond of hot days. And the nights are cold—but one always sleeps well under blankets. And it never rains here—but I despise a country where rain and mud are fashionable. And there are no mosquitoes here—but then I can get along without them. And there are scorpions here—and tarantulas or spiders, as big as a mouse—but I am passionately fond of spiders. Tell them I never liked any country so well before—and my word for it, you will tell them the truth.

A New Vocation
FROM *ROUGHING IT*, BY MARK TWAIN

Sam Clemens's journalism career began with a series of letters written for the Virginia City, Nevada, TERRITORIAL ENTERPRISE in the time he could spare from his various mining ventures. In 1862, when the ENTERPRISE offered him a full-time position, Clemens, with mining putting no money in his pocket, eagerly accepted. The story is that Clemens walked the 150 miles from his camp in Aurora to Virginia City to embark upon his new career. In ROUGHING IT, Twain describes the financial desperation that led him to accept a position he felt little qualified to fill.

N ow in pleasanter days I had amused myself with writing letters to the chief paper of the Territory, the Virginia *Daily Territorial Enterprise,* and had always been surprised when they appeared in print. My good opinion of the editors had steadily declined; for it seemed to me that they might have found something better to fill up with than my literature. I had found a letter in the post office as I came home from the hillside, and finally I opened it. Eureka! (I never did know what Eureka meant, but it seems to be as proper a word to heave in as any when no other that sounds pretty offers.) It was a deliberate offer to me of Twenty-Five Dollars a week to come up to Virginia and be city editor of the *Enterprise.*

I would have challenged the publisher in the "blind lead" days—I wanted to fall down and worship him, now. Twenty-Five Dollars a week—it looked like bloated luxury—a fortune, a sinful and lavish waste of money. But my transports cooled when I thought of my inexperience and consequent unfitness for the position—and straightway, on top of this, my long array of failures rose up before me. Yet if I refused this place I must presently become dependent upon somebody for my bread, a thing necessarily distasteful to a man who had never experienced such a humiliation since he was thirteen years old. Not much to be proud of, since it is so common—but then it was all I had to *be* proud of. So I was scared into being

In the pages of the ENTERPRISE, Clemens wrote often as a reporter of fact, but he found himself more at ease as an inventor of fiction. His humor was lost on many. In a story he called "The Petrified Man," Clemens reported that a body had been discovered in the desert outside town, petrified just like the rock all around it. Clemens described the posture of the body, which astute readers noticed had him thumbing up his nose. Clemens's piece was a subtle hoax, apparently too subtle for a prominent local judge, who, oblivious to Clemens's humor, traveled to the spot to make a personal investigation. When the judge discovered he had been fooled, he was irate and turned on the ENTERPRISE's editors, who in turn reprimanded Clemens for going too far. Clemens, however, was impressed not by the reprimand, but by the power of his words to arouse his readers.

1864

President Abraham Lincoln is reelected despite much opposition and unpopularity in the Union states.

1864

The first newspapers begin publishing in both the North Dakota and Montana Territories.

1864

General Sherman's army of sixty-two thousand Union men leaves the city of Atlanta in flames after their March to the Sea, which left a path of destruction through Georgia. The soldiers continue on to Savannah, which they occupy on December 21.

1865

President Lincoln is inaugurated to his second term as president. In his brief address, met by a respectfully quiet and subdued audience, he urges the country to strive for peace, "with malice toward none, with charity for all."

1865

The Civil War officially ends on April 9 with the surrender of General Robert E. Lee to General Ulysses S. Grant at Appomattox Courthouse, Virginia.

1865

President Lincoln is assassinated on April 12 in Ford's Theatre in Washington, D.C., by Confederate sympathizer John Wilkes Booth. Booth is later captured and executed for his crime.

1865

The SAN FRANCISCO DRAMATIC CHRONICLE is founded by the de Young brothers; MT is an early contributor.

1865

The Thirteenth Amendment to the Constitution ends slavery in the United States.

1865

"Jim Smiley and His Jumping Frog," a short story written by MT, appears in the New York SATURDAY PRESS in November and receives positive reviews.

1866

MT visits the Sandwich Islands (Hawaii) as a correspondent for the Sacramento UNION.

city editor. I would have declined, otherwise. Necessity is the mother of "taking chances." I do not doubt that if, at that time, I had been offered a salary to translate the Talmud from the original Hebrew, I would have accepted—albeit with diffidence and some misgivings—and thrown as much variety into it as I could for the money.

I went up to Virginia and entered upon my new vocation. I was a rusty-looking city editor, I am free to confess—coatless, slouch hat, blue woolen shirt, pantaloons stuffed into boot-tops, whiskered half down to the waist, and the universal navy revolver slung to my belt. But I secured a more Christian costume and discarded the revolver. I had never had occasion to kill anybody, nor ever felt a desire to do so, but had worn the thing in deference to popular sentiment, and in order that I might not, by its absence, be offensively conspicuous and a subject of remark. But the other editors, and all the printers, carried revolvers. I asked the chief editor and proprietor (Mr. Goodman, I will call him, since it describes him as well as any name could do) for some instructions with regard to my duties, and he told me to go all over town and ask all sorts of people all sorts of questions, make notes of the information gained, and write them out for publication.

The ENTERPRISE was called the best newspaper east of California and west of Missouri. It was run by two young editors who saw great promise in Clemens's writing and great potential in his connection to Orion and the territorial government. In 1862, Virginia City was a booming city of forty thousand inhabitants—only five percent of whom were women. There were brothels, saloons, and theatres, along with gunfights and a good measure of western lawlessness. For two years, Clemens covered the territorial legislature and built a reputation as a skilled reporter and a man of strong opinions. Some of these opinions angered the wrong people, however, and in May of 1864 he made a quick exit and headed to California. His time at the ENTERPRISE, despite its poor ending, had been invaluable. It established his reputation as a writer and also gave occasion for him to begin using the pen name Mark Twain. Clemens later claimed that the name was taken from a fellow pilot from his riverboat days, but factual evidence does not support this. Some insist that the name comes from the term in river jargon that indicates the passage from safe, deep water into water two fathoms deep and dangerous for steamboats. Regardless of its origin, the name stuck, and in February of 1863 Sam Clemens became Mark Twain. At right, Clemens during his Virginia City days. Photo The Mark Twain House.

MARK TWAIN IN HAWAII

FROM *MARK TWAIN IN CALIFORNIA*, BY NIGEY LENNON

After his abrupt departure from Virginia City, Clemens found work in San Francisco as a correspondent for the Sacramento UNION *and the San Francisco* MORNING CALL. *His most memorable assignment during his three years in San Francisco was a four-month tour of the Sandwich Islands, now known as the state of Hawaii. Clemens contracted with the* UNION *to write a series of letters describing life and culture on the islands, which were at the time still independent and under the reign of King Kamehameha V. Americans had a voracious appetite for information about these exotic islands, which were becoming increasingly tied to the United States economically and diplomatically. The following account of Clemens's time in Hawaii highlights the importance of the trip in the development of his career and his character.*

On March 7, 1866, he hung over the rail of the *Ajax* as she steamed out of San Francisco harbor, leaning into the crisp, refreshing wind that whipped the wavelets of the Golden Gate into stiff white peaks and caused his bushy red hair to fly wildly about his face. Bret Harte's initial impression of Clemens had been that he was a man "whose general manner was one of supreme indifference to surroundings and circumstances," but nothing could have been further from the truth. Twain was a natural travel writer. Few others would ever be able to equal his sharp eye for detail and the amazing sense of place he possessed after spending only a few hours in a new environment. At the moment, on board the *Ajax*, he was positively glorifying in the notion that he was heading somewhere wild and unknown. Years later, after crisscrossing the globe dozens of times, Twain would lose his appetite for new places, for they would no longer be new to him. But in 1866, as he leaned over the rail of the *Ajax*, travel was a completely fresh experience for him, and he felt as if all the cobwebs of his previous life were blowing away.

He arrived in Honolulu on March 18. From then until he left the Sandwich Islands the following July, he claimed to have enjoyed "half a year's luxurious vagrancy in the islands." This was, of course, one of his typical "stretchers"; his visit lasted only four and a half months, and those months were not exactly frittered away in idleness. During that period, he sent back twenty-five articles to the *Union* which ranged in length from 1,800 to 3,500 words. For each of these, he was paid twenty dollars.

In order to pack the articles full of information, Twain "ransacked the islands, the cataracts and the volcanoes completely." He did this by traveling around the islands on horseback and on foot, passing from island to island on intraisland packets like the wretched *Boomerang*. The *Boomerang*'s route lay between Honolulu and the "big island" of Hawaii, a trip of one hundred and fifty miles. She was a cramped, dingy, derelict craft with minuscule cabins for the first-class passengers such as Twain. In *Roughing It* Twain recalled his first night out aboard the *Boomerang*, lying in a bunk that resembled a coffin and pestered half to death by overly sociable rats, enormous cockroaches with "long quivering antennae and fiery, malignant eyes," and acrobatic fleas who "were throwing double somersaults about my person in the wildest disorder, and taking a bite every time they struck."

Clemens wrote twenty-five letters to the UNION during his trip to Hawaii. His original intention was to turn these letters into a full-length book, but instead he worked the material into sixteen chapters of the book ROUGHING IT, *which blended fact with fiction to tell the story of his entire stay in the western territories. Illustration from* ROUGHING IT, *The Mark Twain House.*

The trip aboard the *Boomerang* was illustrative of the rugged conditions of life Twain found in the islands—conditions that, surprisingly, he endured bravely and even uncomplainingly. The novelty of life in the islands was apparently enough to keep his mind off the discomforts he suffered, although he generally preferred luxury over "roughing it."

He observed the islands' native population at some length and with the greatest of interest, just as he had surveyed local Indian tribes in California and Nevada. In Washoe, he had speculated about the supposedly romantic origins of the Indian name "Tahoe," finally explaining that the name meant nothing more exalted than "grasshopper soup," that perennial favorite of the Paiute Indians. Now, in his articles from the islands, Twain had a great deal to say about the islands' natives, or "Kanakas" as they were called. One thing Twain observed was that due to the warm climate of the islands, the Kanakas wore very little clothing. The nineteenth century got to tugging at him a little, reminding him that only savages don't have an inborn sense of modesty, but Twain's basic nature found the seminudity of the Kanakas to be a charming and (in view of the climate) a logical thing. . . .

Twain soon discovered that his reputation as the most popular writer in San Francisco had preceded him to the islands; everywhere he went, he found a hearty welcome from his fellow Americans. In the cool, shady, stately homes where he stayed, on plantations as well as in the islands' few cities, he found the company exceedingly cordial. The relaxed pace of life enjoyed by the island dwellers appeared to him to be a tonic for stress as well as a promoter of tranquility and contentment. In his notebook, he observed that he saw "no careworn or eager, anxious faces in this land of happy contentment. God, what a contrast with California and the Washoe!" And, "They *live* in the Sandwich Islands—no rush, no worry—merchant goes down to his store like a gentleman at nine—goes home at four and *thinks no more* of business till next day. Damned San F. style of wearing out life."

Perhaps he was unaware of it, but his view of the islands was hardly a complete one. The Sandwich Islands expedition occurred at a point in Twain's life when he had not yet become anti–imperialistic, as he would in later years. In fact, as he talked with the American plantation owners, he became firmly convinced that the United States should annex the Sandwich Islands in order to reap the benefits of the islands' bountiful sugar and coffee crops and other resources. Although he had taken the side of the Chinese immigrant workers in San Francisco, he seemed to see no contradiction between his earlier and present opinions when he viewed the Chinese laborers who toiled in the sugar cane fields as a fine source of cheap, hard-working manpower that made the Hawaiian sugar industry all the more promising for the United States.

Despite his perennial disenchantment with organized religion, Twain also had nothing especially scathing to say about the American missionaries who had come to the islands in the earlier part of the century, and who were continuing their self-appointed task of "civilizing" the Kanakas as only they knew how. Later, Twain would change his attitude about the missionaries—in relatively short order, as a matter of fact—but during his stay in the islands he only praised them for eradicating native superstition, without stopping to think what they had replaced that superstition *with*.

The volcano of Kilauea was still active during Twain's sojourn in the islands, and he had heard so much about it that he determined to get as close to its explosive central crater as possible. With an equally reckless fellow named Marlette, who was familiar with the multifarious nooks and crannies of the mammoth fire mountain, Twain walked directly across the floor of the volcano's crater by night, dashing lightly over sheets of fiery lava that flowed around his feet, and leaping across wide crevices from which the molten fire trapped inside emitted a baleful red glow.

At one point, his guide shouted for him to stop. "I never stopped quicker in my life," wrote Twain in *Roughing It*. "I asked what the matter was. He said we were out of the path. He said we must not go on until we found it again, for we were surrounded with beds of rotten lava, through which we could easily break and plunge down 1,000 feet. I thought 800 would answer for me, and was about to say so, when Marlette partly proved his statement, crushing through and disappearing to his arm-pits."

Marlette got out all right, and the two explorers proceeded to spend the rest of the night gazing down into the hellish depths of the red-hot crater. This was an experience that Twain relished intensely and that he remembered vividly for the rest of his life, often retelling it in such a way that it struck awe and wonder into the hearts of visitors. The idea of risking his neck to peer into the very depths of a live and malevolent volcano was a notion that thrilled Twain to the depths of his soul.

At the end of June he returned to Honolulu from his wanderings, intending to rest for a while and nurse the saddle boils he had accumulated during his travels on horseback around the islands. He was lying in bed in his hotel room in Honolulu when he received a message from some very august personages indeed, saying that they were going to pay him a call at his hotel the next morning.

Twain was shaken up considerably at this news, for the party was headed up by His Excellency Anson Burlingame, who had just arrived on the *Ajax* from San Francisco en route to a diplomatic post as American minister to China. There were also some other American diplomats who were traveling to China with Burlingame—Generals Van Valkenberg and Rumsey, respectively, as well as Burlingame's eighteen-year-old son, Edward. Clemens was no stranger to the workings of politics, nor was he particularly sentimental when it came to the bloated aristocrats of political pomp. Nonetheless, after hearing through channels in Honolulu that Burlingame's son Edward was a big fan of "The Jumping Frog" and wanted very much to meet its author, he positively beamed. However, he realized that, saddle boils or no saddle boils, it would be quite unseemly to oblige such an exalted group to call on him in his hotel room, so the next morning he dragged himself painfully out of bed, applied a pair of pants as gingerly as he could over the affected area, and drove with all haste to the house belonging to the American minister to the Sandwich Islands, where Burlingame and company were quartered.

His visit was an unqualified success, for he was careful to pull out all the stops and make himself thoroughly agreeable and amusing, and the diplomats found his charm irresistible. For his part, Twain was considerably impressed by Anson Burlingame, and remained so throughout his life. Burlingame gave him a piece of advice that the Sagebrush Bohemian saw fit to take to heart, for better or for worse: "You have great ability; I believe you have genius. What you need now is the refinement of association. Seek companionship among men of superior intellect and character. Refine yourself and your work. Never affiliate with inferiors; always climb."

When he returned to California from Hawaii, with information about his trip in great demand, Clemens hit upon an idea that would shape his career for the remainder of his life. On October 2, 1866, Clemens took the stage before a packed lecture hall and delivered a humorous and colorful account of his experiences in the Sandwich Islands. Nearly paralyzed by fear before the lecture began, he completed it to loud applause and walked off the platform certain that lecturing would play a larger role in his future.

A full and attentive audience assembled at the Cooper Institute last evening to listen to the recital of Mark Twain's experiences in the Sandwich islands. Nearly everyone present came prepared for considerable provocation for enjoyable laughter, and from the appearance of the mirthful faces leaving the hall at the conclusion of the lecture, but few were disappointed, and it is not too much to say that seldom has so large an audience been so uniformly pleased as the one that listened to Mark Twain's quaint remarks last evening. The large hall of the union was filled to its utmost capacity by fully two thousand persons, which fact spoke well for the brilliant reputation of the lecturer and his future success. Mr. Twain's style is a quaint one, both in manner and method, and throughout his discourse he managed to keep on the right side of his audience and frequently convulsed it with hearty laughter. Some of the anecdotes related were wittily told, and so embellished as to be doubly enjoyed by his hearers. While the speaker made some very amusing comments on the habits and customs of the Sandwich Islanders, he stated that all the facts related by him were strictly true. The speaker gave the American missionaries great credit for their work in civilizing and converting the Islanders, and spoke of the singular fact that the descendants of these missionaries have no stain upon their moral character, being exemplary citizens.

During his description of the topography of the Sandwich Islands, the lecturer surprised his hearers by a graphic and eloquent description of the eruption of the great volcano which occurred in 1840, and his language was loudly applauded.

Judging from the success achieved by the lecturer last evening, he should repeat the experiment at an early day.

THE NEW YORK TIMES, 1866

THE JUMPING FROG STORY

FROM "JIM SMILEY AND HIS JUMPING FROG," BY MARK TWAIN

"Jim Smiley and His Jumping Frog" was the story that made the name Mark Twain famous. Clemens had gained renown under his pseudonym in the West, particularly in Nevada and California, but this simple story about a too-confident gambler who is finally undone by a clever stranger appeared in the SATURDAY PRESS, in New York City, and made Mark Twain known to readers on both coasts. The story was published November 18, 1865. It later appeared under the names "The Notorious Jumping Frog of Calaveras County" and "The Celebrated Jumping Frog of Calaveras County." Above, a portrait of Mark Twain during his California days. Photo The Mark Twain House.

Clemens created his "jumping frog story" from a tale told to him around a campfire in a California mining town. He recorded the outline of the story in his notebook and predicted that if he could come up with a written version of the story to match the one he'd heard, the frog would "jump around the world." His confidence wavered, however. In a letter to Orion, Clemens spoke of his call to what he characterized as "low" humorous literature. He would give up his larger ambitions, he wrote, and turn his attention to "seriously scribbling to excite the laughter of God's creatures. Poor, pitiful business!"

Well, thish-yer Smiley had rat-terriers and chicken cocks, and tom-cats, and all them kind of things, till you couldn't rest, and you couldn't fetch nothing for him to bet on but he'd match you. He ketched a frog one day and took him home and said he cal'lated to educate him; and so he never done nothing for three months but set in his back yard and learn that frog to jump. And you bet you he *did* learn him, too. He'd give him a little hunch behind, and the next minute you'd see that frog whirling in the air like a doughnut—see him turn one summerset, or maybe a couple, if he got a good start, and come down flat-footed and all right, like a cat. He got him up so in the matter of ketching flies, and kept him in practice so constant, that he'd nail a fly every time as far as he could see him. Smiley said all a frog wanted was education, and he could do most anything—and I believe him. Why, I've seen him set Dan'l Webster down here on this floor—Dan'l Webster was the name of the frog—and sing out, "Flies! Dan'l, flies," and quicker'n you could wink, he'd spring straight up, and snake a fly off'n the counter there, and flop down on the floor again as solid as a gob of mud, and fall to scratching the side of his head with his hind foot as indifferent as if he hadn't no idea he'd done any more'n any frog might do. You never see a frog so modest and straightfor'ard as he was, for all he was so gifted. And when it come to fair-and-square jumping on a dead level, he could get over more ground at one straddle than any animal of his breed you ever see. Jumping on a dead level was his strong suit, you understand, and when it come to that, Smiley would ante up money on him as long as he had a red. Smiley was monstrous proud of his frog, and well he might be, for fellers that had travelled and ben everywheres all said he laid over any frog that ever *they* see.

Well, Smiley kept the beast in a little lattice box, and he used to fetch him down town sometimes and lay for a bet. One day a feller—a stranger in the camp, he was—come across him with his box, and says:

"What might it be that you've got in the box?"

And Smiley says, sorter indifferent like, "It might be a parrot, or it might be a canary, maybe, but it ain't—it's only just a frog."

And the feller took it, and looked at it careful, and turned it round this way and that, and says, "H'm—so 'tis. Well, what's *he* good for?"

"Well," Smiley says, easy and careless, "He's good enough for *one* thing I should judge—he can out-jump ary frog in Calaveras county."

The feller took the box again, and took another long, particular look, and give it back to

Smiley and says, very deliberate, "Well—I don't see no points about that frog that's any better'n any other frog."

"Maybe you don't," Smiley says. "Maybe you understand frogs, and maybe you don't understand 'em; maybe you've had experience, and maybe you ain't only a amature, as it were. Anyways, I've got *my* opinion, and I'll resk forty dollars that he can outjump ary frog in Calaveras county."

And the feller studied a minute, and then says, kinder sad, like, "Well—I'm only a stranger here, and I ain't got no frog—but if I had a frog I'd bet you."

And then Smiley says, "That's all right—that's all right—if you'll hold my box a minute I'll go and get you a frog;" and so the feller took the box, and put up his forty dollars along with Smiley's, and set down to wait.

So he set there a good while thinking and thinking to hisself, and then he got the frog out and prized his mouth open and took a teaspoon and filled him full of quail-shot—filled him pretty near up to his chin—and set him on the floor. Smiley he went out to the swamp and slopped around in the mud for a long time, and finally he ketched a frog and fetched him in and give him to this feller and says:

"Now if you're ready, set him alongside of Dan'l, with his forepaws just even with Dan'l's, and I'll give the word." Then he says, "one—two—three—jump!" and him and the feller touched up the frogs from behind, and the new frog hopped off lively, but Dan'l give a heave, and hysted up his shoulders—so—like a Frenchman, but it wasn't no use—he couldn't budge; he was planted as solid as a anvil, and he couldn't no more stir than if he was anchored out. Smiley was a good deal surprised, and he was disgusted too, but he didn't have no idea what the matter was, of course.

The feller took the money and started away, and when he was going out at the door he sorter jerked his thumb over his shoulder—this way—at Dan'l, and says again, very deliberate, "Well—*I* don't see no points about that frog that's any better'n any other frog."

Smiley he stood scratching his head and looking down at Dan'l a long time, and at last he says, "I do wonder what in the nation that frog throwed off for—I wonder if there ain't something the matter with him—he 'pears to look mighty baggy, somehow"—and he ketched Dan'l by the nap of the neck, and lifted him up and says, "Why blame my cats if he don't weigh five pound"—and turned him upside down, and he belched out about a double-handful of shot. And then he see how it was, and he was the maddest man—he set the frog down and took out after that feller, but he never ketched him. And—

[Here Simon Wheeler heard his name called from the frontyard, and got up to go and see what was wanted.] And turning to me as he moved away, he said: "Just sit where you are, stranger, and rest easy—I ain't going to be gone a second."

But by your leave, I did not think that a continuation of the history of the enterprising vagabond Jim Smiley would be likely to afford me much information concerning the Rev. Leonidas W. Smiley, and so I started away. . . .

I met the sociable Wheeler returning, and he buttonholed me and recommenced:

"Well, thish-yer Smiley had a yaller one-eyed cow that didn't have no tail only just a short stump like a bannanner, and—"

"O, curse Smiley and his afflicted cow!" I muttered, good-naturedly, and bidding the old gentleman good-day, I departed.

In a handsomely printed and tastefully bound little volume, called the Jumping Frog, which is the initial venture of Mr. C. H. Webb as a publisher, "Mark Twain" presents himself as a candidate for the honors of a humorist. "Mark Twain" is, we believe, the nom de plume of Mr. SAMUEL CLEMENS, who, although a Missourian by birth, has for the last year had his residence in California. There his contributions to the weekly journals secured him a wide popularity, and this volume serves to introduce him to the lovers of humor in the Atlantic states. The sketch from which the book takes its name was first published several years ago, and at that time was widely circulated through the newspapers. It is a fair specimen of the whimsical fancies in which the book abounds, and, although there are other sketches nearly equal to it in merit, it is appropriately assigned the leading place because it has done more than any other single paper to secure for the writer whatever reputation he may have. "Mark Twain" differs from other recent writers of his class in not resorting to the adventitious aid of bad spelling to make his jokes seem more absurd, and this is, of course, decidedly in his favor. There is a great deal of quaint humor and much pithy wisdom in his writings, and their own merit, as well as the attractive style in which they are produced, must secure them a popularity which will bring its own profit. . . .

from a review of THE JUMPING FROG, THE NEW YORK TIMES, *May 1, 1867*

THE TOMB OF ADAM

FROM *THE INNOCENTS ABROAD*, BY MARK TWAIN

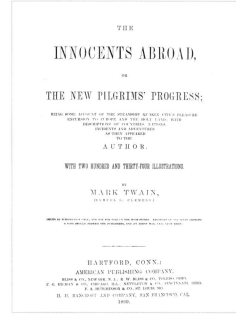

THE INNOCENTS ABROAD *appeared in 1869 with the subtitle* THE NEW PILGRIMS' PROGRESS; BEING SOME ACCOUNT OF THE STEAMSHIP QUAKER CITY'S PLEASURE EXCURSION TO EUROPE AND THE HOLY LAND. *It was the first full-length book published under the name Mark Twain, and it received generally favorable reviews for its humorous and original blend of fact and fiction in its description of the 164 days at sea and on land during the* QUAKER CITY *trip. Above, the title page from* THE INNOCENTS ABROAD. *Photo The Mark Twain House.*

Clemens left California in 1867 as a traveling correspondent for the San Francisco ALTA CALIFORNIA. *His assignment was an excursion aboard the steamboat* QUAKER CITY *as one of a group of paying passengers signed on to tour the Mediterranean and the Holy Land with the leaders of Reverend Henry Ward Beecher's Brooklyn, New York, church. The ship carried nearly seventy passengers, for the most part wealthy American Protestants on what was to be a pleasure cruise with a dose of education. Clemens contracted with the* ALTA *to write a series of letters from the* QUAKER CITY *describing the sights and experiences. The idea of transforming these letters into a book did not come about until after the voyage was complete. In* THE INNOCENTS ABROAD, *Mark Twain brought the American people a new type of travel book—one which did not ask them to humble themselves in front of the great sights and cities of the Old World, but instead viewed the monuments of Europe and the Holy Land with a sense of humor and a liberal dose of irreverence.*

The Greek chapel is the most roomy, the richest and the showiest chapel in the Church of the Holy Sepulchre. Its altar, like that of all the Greek churches, is a lofty screen that extends clear across the chapel, and is gorgeous with gilding and pictures. The numerous lamps that hang before it are of gold and silver, and cost great sums.

But the feature of the place is a short column that rises from the middle of the marble pavement of the chapel and marks the exact *center of the earth*. The most reliable traditions tell us that this was known to be the earth's center, ages ago, and that when Christ was upon earth he set all doubts upon the subject at rest forever by stating with his own lips that the tradition was correct. Remember, he said that that particular column stood upon the center of the world. If the center of the world changes, the column changes its position accordingly. This column has moved three different times of its own accord. This is because, in great convulsions of nature, at three different times, masses of the earth—whole ranges of mountains, probably—have flown off into space, thus lessening the diameter of the earth and changing the exact locality of its center by a point or two. This is a very curious and interesting circumstance, and is a withering rebuke to those philosophers who would make us believe that it is not possible for any portion of the earth to fly off into space.

To satisfy himself that this spot was really the center of the earth, a skeptic once paid well for the privilege of ascending to the dome of the church to see if the sun gave him a shadow at noon. He came down perfectly convinced. The day was very cloudy and the sun threw no shadows at all; but the man was satisfied that if the sun had come out and made shadows it could not have made any for him. Proofs like these are not to be aside by the idle tongues of cavilers. To such as are not bigoted and are willing to be convinced, they carry a conviction that nothing can ever shake.

If even greater proofs than those I have mentioned are wanted, to satisfy the headstrong and the foolish that this is the genuine center of the earth, they are here. The greatest of them lies in the fact that from under this very column was taken the *dust from which Adam was made.* This can surely be regarded in the light of a settler. It is not likely that the original first man would have been made from an inferior quality of earth when it was entirely convenient to get first quality from the world's center. This will strike any reflecting mind forcibly. That Adam was formed of dirt procured in this very spot is amply proven by the fact that in six thousand years no man has ever been able to prove that the dirt was *not* procured here whereof he was made.

It is a singular circumstance that right under the roof of this same great church, and not far away from that illustrious column, Adam himself, the father of the human race, lies buried. There is no question that he is actually buried in the grave which is pointed out as his—there can be none—because it has never yet been proven that that grave is not the grave in which he is buried.

The tomb of Adam! How touching it was, here in a land of strangers, far away from home and friends and all who cared for me, thus to discover the grave of a blood relation. True, a distant one, but still a relation. The unerring instinct of nature thrilled its recognition. The fountain of my filial affection was stirred to its profoundest depths, and I gave way to tumultuous emotion. I leaned upon a pillar and burst into tears. I deem it no shame to have wept over the grave of my poor dead relative. Let him who would sneer at my emotion close this volume here, for he will find little to his taste in my journeyings through Holy Land. Noble old man—he did not live to see me—he did not live to see his child. And I—I—alas, I did not live to see *him*. Weighed down by sorrow and disappointment, he died before I was born—six thousand brief summers before I was born. But let us try to bear it with fortitude. Let us trust that he is better off where he is. Let us take comfort in the thought that his loss is our eternal gain.

The QUAKER CITY *is pictured in rough seas in the frontispiece from the book that Clemens eventually wrote about the trip,* THE INNOCENTS ABROAD. *Illustration The Mark Twain House.*

I know I ought to write oftener (just got your last,) & more fully, but I can not overcome my repugnance to telling what I am doing or what I expect to do or propose to do. Then, what have I left to write about? Manifestly nothing.

It isn't any use for me to talk about the voyage, because I can have no faith in that voyage or any other voyage till the ship is under way. How do I know she will ever sail? My passage is paid, & if the ship sails, I sail in her—but I make no calculations, have bought no cigars, no sea-going clothing,—have made no preparation whatever—shall not pack my trunk till the morning we sail. Yet my hands are full of what I am going to do the day before we sail—& what isn't done that day will go undone.

All I do know or feel, is, that I am wild with impatience to move—move—Move! Half a dozen times I have wished I had sailed long ago in some ship that wasn't going to keep me chained here to chafe for lagging ages while she got ready to go. Curse the endless delays! They always kill me—they make me neglect every duty & then I have a conscience that tears me like a wild beast. I wish I never had to stop anywhere a month. I do more mean things, the moment I get a chance to fold my hands & sit down than ever I can get forgiveness for.

Yes, we are to meet at Mr Beach's next Thursday night & I suppose we shall have to be gotten up regardless of expense, in swallow-tails, white kids & everything en régle.

I am resigned to Rev. Mr. Hutchinson's or anybody's else's supervision. I don't mind it. I am fixed. I have got a splendid, immoral, tobacco-smoking, wine-drinking, godless room-mate who is as good & true & right-minded a man as ever lived—a man whose blameless conduct & example will always be an eloquent sermon to all who shall come within their influence. But send on the professional preachers—there are none I like better to converse with—if they ain't narrow minded & bigoted they make good companions.

I asked them to send the N.Y. Weekly to you—no charge. I am not going to write for it—like all other papers that pay one splendidly, it circulates among stupid people & the canaille. I have made no arrangement with any New York paper—I will see about that Monday or Tuesday.

Samuel Clemens, from a letter from to his family,
June 1, 1867

Mark Twain

HARTFORD, FAMILY, FAME
1867–1890

Although mention of the name Mark Twain immediately brings to mind images of Hannibal, Missouri, and the Mississippi River, it was half a continent away, in Hartford, Connecticut, that Sam Clemens lived longer than in any other single place; and it was while Clemens was a Hartford resident that his greatest writing was done. Drawn to the city by its beauty, its proximity to both New York and Boston, and by the community of writers and friends living there in a place known as Nook Farm, Clemens and his wife Olivia settled in Hartford in 1871. The two decades that followed were a time of productivity and happiness. Sam and Livy raised their three daughters, and he, under the pen name Mark Twain, published a string of successful novels, bringing to life such memorable characters as Tom Sawyer and Huckleberry Finn. In Hartford in the 1870s and 1880s, Clemens was happy, successful, and, for a time, content.

Illustration at right by Norman Rockwell from ADVENTURES OF
HUCKLEBERRY FINN, *1940 edition*

THE FORTUNE OF MY LIFE

FROM *MR. CLEMENS AND MARK TWAIN*, BY JUSTIN KAPLAN

1867

MT is a passenger aboard the QUAKER CITY for a trip through the Mediterranean and the Holy Land.

1867

MT meets his future wife, Olivia Langdon, the sister of a fellow QUAKER CITY passenger.

1868

President Andrew Johnson is impeached for violating the Tenure of Office Act by dismissing Secretary of War Edwin Stanton. The impeachment is pushed by a group of Republican congressmen angry at Johnson's Reconstruction policies. Johnson is acquitted when the vote falls one short of the two-thirds majority needed for conviction.

1868

The Fourteenth Amendment, which grants citizenship to all persons born or naturalized in the United States, most importantly the former slaves, is passed in July.

1868

Ulysses S. Grant is elected president of the United States. Seven hundred thousand of the nearly six million votes are cast by former black slaves.

1868

MT begins an extended lecture tour that takes him through Nevada and California and, later, throughout the Northeast and Midwest.

1869

The Fifteenth Amendment, adopted in April, grants suffrage to American citizens regardless of race, color, or previous condition of servitude. One group not included is American women; in May, the National Woman Suffrage Association is founded by Elizabeth Cady Stanton and Susan B. Anthony.

1869

The Union and Pacific railroads meet in Utah, connecting the nation's two coasts by rail.

1869

THE INNOCENTS ABROAD by MT is published in July.

Clemens often claimed that he fell in love with Olivia Langdon the instant he saw the miniature picture of her that her brother Charles carried with him on the QUAKER CITY *excursion. Whether this is fact or fabrication, Clemens and Langdon met in December of 1867, shortly after the* QUAKER CITY *trip, and married a little over two years later. They were an unlikely match. He was rough and profane, accustomed to life on steamboats and on the western frontier. She was refined and frail, the product of a loving but sheltered upbringing. Here, Justin Kaplan describes their first meeting in New York City in 1867.*

Clemens met her around Christmas time 1867. He was in New York on a two-week visit with Slote, and was invited by Charley Langdon to meet his sister and his parents at the St. Nicholas Hotel, once the city's grandest palace of gold leaf and mirrors but now subsided into ultra-respectability. Clemens called on the Langdons on December 27 and was introduced to Livy. On New Year's Eve he accompanied her to Charles Dickens' reading at Steinway Hall. Among but above the other attractions of New York, Dickens had drawn the Langdons down from Elmira as he had drawn enormous crowds, five thousand at a time, who lined up in front of ticket offices before dawn on winter mornings. Speculators were riding high; Dickens' novels were selling by the tens of thousands; and the day after he arrived all but two of the nineteen hundred copies of his work in the Mercantile Library were out on loan. For all his criticism of America and his careful avoidance during the Civil War of any expression of support for the Union side, Dickens was still a Northern hero, a demigod even for abolitionists like the Langdons. The circumstances of the evening Sam Clemens spent with his future wife were appropriate. This was the valedictory reading tour of a towering literary personality, a hero of the mass audience which would soon elevate the newcomer, Mark Twain, also a great public reader as well as an actor *manqué,* to an analogous height. Despite his awe of Dickens, "this puissant god," Clemens confessed that he was disappointed: the readings from *David Copperfield* struck him as monotonous, the pathos as purely verbal, "glittering frostwork, with no heart." Dickens mumbled, and the audience, though eager and intelligent, managed to remain unexcited. So Clemens reported to his California paper. He also reported, "I am proud to observe that there was a beautiful young lady with me—a highly respectable young white woman." In an account which he dictated nearly forty years later he fitted that evening with Livy into a characteristic nexus of motives, for, at the height of his Hartford years with her, love, happiness, literary fame, and money had become convertible currency. Charles Dickens made $200,000 from his readings that season, Clemens recalled, but that one evening with Livy "made the fortune of my life—not in dollars, I am not thinking of dollars; it made the real fortune of my life in that it made the happiness of my life."

The next day Clemens paid Livy a New Year's call at the house of her friend Mrs. Berry. There, amidst the Moorish décor which marked his hostess as a lady of wealth and discrimination, he remained the entire day and part of the evening. With Livy was another friend, Alice

Hooker, daughter of the disapproving Hookers of Hartford and niece of the two Beecher clergymen. Despite the gaiety of the occasion, there was little or no alcohol and a great deal of propriety, and although Clemens spent thirteen hours at this marathon reception, he probably got to know the beautiful Miss Hooker at least as well as he could have known the "sweet and timid and lovely" twenty-two-year-old Livy. For, as he wholly idealized her, she was angelic, disembodied. The distance between them was too great for him to dare think of love; reverent worship, at best the grave affection of brother for sister, alone was possible. "You seemed to my bewildered vision a visiting *Spirit* from the upper air," he recalled a year later, "*not* a creature of common human clay, to be profaned by the *love* of such as I." After three meetings with Livy he had not progressed far enough to dare to write to her, and the one overt carry-over was an invitation from the Langdons to visit them in Elmira. He had seen her ivory miniature in September 1867; he met her at the turn of the year; he did not pay his visit to Elmira until August 1868; and before then, in February, he considered a diplomatic post in China which would keep him out of the country for a long time. Wooing her had not yet become even a possibility for him, and beyond a mention in one of his letters home—"Charlie Langdon's sister was there (beautiful girl)"—Livy vanishes from his record for over half a year. . . .

The Langdons were a family of wealth and culture, among the most respected citizens of their hometown of Elmira, New York. They did not drink, they did not smoke, and they joined together nightly in family prayers and hymn singing. Clemens was to them at first a rough and worrisome, albeit enjoyable, character; eventually, his devotion to Livy and his measurable personal charm won them over. For Livy, Clemens vowed he would give up drinking, smoking, and swearing. In truth, although their marriage lasted thirty-four years, Clemens never did reform; they remained the opposites of their initial attraction. Livy Clemens always disliked hearing her husband described as a humorist. "Poor girl," Clemens wrote of his wife to a friend, "anybody who could convince her that I was not a humorist would secure her eternal gratitude." At left, Olivia Langdon in 1869. Photo The Mark Twain Memorial.

SAM AND LIVY

FROM *MR. CLEMENS AND MARK TWAIN*, BY JUSTIN KAPLAN

1869

John Wesley Powell, a wounded Civil War veteran, is first to navigate the Colorado River through the Grand Canyon.

1870

In February, MT and Olivia Langdon are married in Elmira, New York.

1870

Senator Hiram Revels of Mississippi becomes the first black American in the Senate; Joseph Rainey of South Carolina also enters Congress as the first black member of the House of Representatives.

1870

MT's first child, a son named Langdon, is born on November 7.

1871

MT and family rent a house in the Nook Farm community in Hartford, Connecticut.

1872

ROUGHING It *by MT is published in February.*

1872

Susy Clemens, MT's second child, is born on March 19.

1872

Langdon Clemens, MT's only son, dies on June 2.

1872

MT travels to England alone; he remains there for three months.

1873

MT buys land for a house at Nook Farm.

1873

The failure of the brokerage firm financing the Northern Pacific Railroad sparks a financial panic that closes the stock exchange for ten days in September. In the years that follow, over ten thousand American businesses fail due to the resulting depression.

Marrying Olivia Langdon brought Clemens into a world entirely new to him—the world of eastern culture and refinement, an upper-middle class society light years removed from the Mississippi River culture of his youth. Clemens eagerly embraced Livy's world as his own, and for a time he prospered in Hartford society; only many years later would he become uncomfortable within its boundaries.

There were carriage rides in the city and in the hills above, walks in the Langdon garden, leisurely visiting. Evenings there were prayers and hymns in the parlor, and Clemens also sang, in his clear tenor voice, the spirituals and jubilees his uncle's slaves had taught him, strange music in the North. In this household, "the pleasantest family I ever knew," Clemens was for a while idyllically and unsuspectingly happy, and he fancied he was "quite a pleasant addition to the family circle." (A half year later Livy hurt his feelings bitterly, set him to moping about rejection and snubbing, by telling him that at one point during his first visit the family had begun to wish that he would leave.) And quite as unsuspecting were the Langdon parents, hospitable, delighted (at first) with their unusual visitor. They had not yet admitted to themselves the possibility of losing Livy to any man, least of all to Sam Clemens. He was ten years older than Livy, older still in the sights he had seen and the things he had done, Othello wooing Desdemona with tales of travels and dangers. The people Clemens had known in Hannibal, on the river, and in the West were scarcely less foreign to Livy than Othello's cannibals and men whose heads grew beneath their shoulders.

Livy was beautiful. Her black hair was drawn smooth over her forehead, framing her cameo face and dark eyes. Her smile, Howells remembered, was of "angelic tenderness," and myopia gave her a look of musing intensity. She was gentle, calm, spiritual, and refined, qualities which Clemens idealized in her and which he found all the more compelling for their contrast to his Western experience. But she also had "the heart-free laugh of a girl," he said, and he sensed in her, and later discovered, an immense capacity for giving and receiving affection. "I was born *reserved* as to endearments of speech and caresses," he wrote in his autobiography. He remembered only one kiss in his family, when John Marshall Clemens on his deathbed kissed Pamela; kissing was rare in Hannibal and generally "ended with courtship—along with the deadly piano-playing of that day." Livy "poured out her prodigal affections in kisses and caresses and in a vocabulary of endearments whose profusion was always an astonishment to me." Yet even after they were engaged the name "Sam" came from her only with the greatest difficulty, as if it represented aspects of that past of his she could never share. She was slow to grasp a joke, but he saw this as a challenge and enjoyed it, and for her benefit he patiently annotated a passage from Holmes's *Autocrat*, "That is a joke, my literal Livy." Her "gentle gravities" sometimes made him laugh. She was timid, often frightened, and when thunder and lightning came she hid in a closet. Yet, invested by him with a power she hardly suspected, when she spoke the word "disapprove" it had, he said, the force of another person's "damn." She disapproved of drinking, smoking, swearing, and, for a while, humorists.

He was in love with Livy, he wanted to marry her more than he had ever wanted any-thing in his life, and he found the pace of a conventional genteel courtship much too slow for him. After less than two weeks in the Langdon house he abandoned the reserve he was born with and proposed to her, and she said no. Early in September, on his last night in Elmira, he consolidated his forces behind the original line of battle. "I do not regret that I have loved you, still love you, and shall always love you," he wrote in the first of nearly two hundred love letters (a mass of manuscript as long as a subscription book) before their marriage in February 1870. He would be able to bear the bitterest "grief, disaster, and disappointment" of his life provided "you will let me freight my speeches to you with simply the sacred love a brother bears to a sis-ter." To save him from becoming forever a "homeless vagabond," he invited Livy, as he had invited Mary Fairbanks, to supervise his regeneration. He begged her to scold and correct him, to lecture him on the sin of smoking, to send him texts from the New Testament, to tell him about Thomas K. Beecher's sermon on Sunday, to send him Henry Ward Beecher's sermon pamphlets.

He courted her by offering in all sincerity to make over his character and habits to suit her standards. Less than a year after they were married he said in half-jest, "I would deprive myself of sugar in my coffee if she wished it, or quit wearing socks if she thought them immoral." Yet he eventually withdrew many of the important concessions he made to her, and he most often had his way about things, even though he enjoyed and exploited playing the role of a man under his wife's thumb. During his courtship he took the oath, but within a few years of their marriage Livy herself was drinking beer before going to bed and he was drinking cocktails of Scotch, lemon, sugar, and Angostura bitters before breakfast as well as dinner and also hot whiskeys at night. "I believe in you, even as I believe in the Savior," he told her early in his courtship, but he went on to explain that his faith was "as simple and unquestioning as the faith of a devotee in the idol he wor-ships." After such romantic paganism it is not surprising that he never became a Christian, and that she eventually became an unbeliever. She reigned, but she did not rule. Nevertheless, within five years of their marriage, Sam Clemens the bohemian and vagabond had undergone a thorough transformation. He embraced upper-middle-class values. He became a gentleman, and for a while an Anglophile who despised the raw democracy which bred him and the corruption and coarse-ness he saw all around him. He was the antithesis of Walt Whitman, also sea-changed in his thir-ties, for Clemens began to find himself as a writer by joining the social order instead of freeing himself from it; only later, when the mature artist came in conflict with the Victorian gentleman of property, did Clemens realize he had been scarred by his concessions. The journalist Walter Whitman became the poet Walt, but Sam became Samuel L. Clemens. He had known Whitman's open road long enough, and what he wanted was home. "The idol is the measure of the worship-per," said James Russell Lowell, and in choosing his idol Clemens chose his transformations as well. They were not forced on him by Olivia Langdon, who, although she had his love, also had what was only an instructed proxy from him. More than a year before he even saw her picture he had already, in some advice given him by Anson Burlingame, the American minister to China, glimpsed his eventual goals. "What you need now is the refinement of association," Burlingame had said somewhat pointedly after Clemens had got tight in Honolulu. "Refine yourself and your work. Never affiliate with inferiors; always *climb*."

The impulse is strong upon me to say to you how grateful I am to you and to all of you, for the patience, the consideration & the unfailing kindness which has been shown me ever since I came within the shadow of this roof, and which has made the past fortnight the sole period of my life unmarred by a regret. Unmarred by a regret. I say it deliberately. For I do not regret that I have loved you, still love & shall always love you. I accept the situation, uncomplainingly, hard as it is. Of old I am acquainted with grief, disaster & disappoint-ment, & have borne these troubles as became a man. So, also, I shall bear this last & bitterest, even though it break my heart. I would not dishonor this worthiest love that has yet been born within me by any puerile thought, or word, or deed. It is better to have loved & lost you than that my life should have remained forever the blank it was before. For once, at least, in the idle years that have drifted over me, I have seen the world all beautiful, & known what it was to hope. For once I have known what it was to feel my sluggish pulses stir with a living ambition. The world that was so beautiful, is dark again; the hope that shone as the sun, is gone; the brave ambition is dead. Yet I say again, it is better for me that I have loved & do love you; that with more than Eastern devotion I worship you; that I lay down all of my life that is worth the living, upon this hopeless altar where no fires of love shall descend to consume it. If you could but—

But no more of this. I have said it only from that impulse which drives men to speak of great calami-ties which have befallen them, & so seek relief. I could not say it to give you pain. The words are spo-ken, & they have fallen upon forgiving ears. For your dear sake my tongue & my pen are now forbidden to repeat them ever again.

And so, henceforward, I claim only that you will let me freight my speeches to you with simply the sacred love a brother bears to a sister. I ask that you will write to me sometimes, as to a friend whom you feel will do all that a man may to be worthy of your friendship—or as to a brother whom you know will hold his sister's honor as dearly as his own, her wishes as his law, her pure judgements above his blinded worldly wisdom. Being adrift, now, & rudderless, my voyage promises ill; but while the friendly beacon of your sisterly love beams, though never so faintly through the fogs & the mists, I cannot be hopelessly wrecked. . . .

Samuel Clemens, from a letter to Olivia Langdon, September 7 and 8, 1868

Precious, Peerless, Matchless girl
Samuel Clemens, from a letter to Olivia Langdon, December 31, 1868

Clemens spent much of his courtship and engagement on lecture tour and thus separated from Livy. They kept in close touch, however, through regular correspondence. In the excerpt below, from a letter written on New Year's Eve, 1868, Clemens thanks Livy for directing him onto a new and happy path and eagerly looks forward to their future together.

Your Christmas letter gave me *so much* pleasure, Livy—& some pain—because *you* had suffered. It breaks my heart to see you suffer, whether it be at the thought of leaving your good home, or for *any* cause. And yet I want you to keep no sorrow of yours from me—I would share your griefs & your heart-aches as well as your joys—I would bear *all* your heart-aches myself, & place myself between you & sorrow, taking all your troubles upon myself & shielding you from all the ills of life, if I only could. But since it is impossible, let me at least suffer *with* you, Livy. Do not grieve, Livy, but look at the pleasant side of the picture. . . . Cheer up—cheer up you precious, peerless, matchless girl—& say again you love me half as well as I love you. Such words *will* come reluctantly from that pen of yours, do what I can to coax them—but say them *anyhow*, Livy, for I love to read them as much as you hate to write them! And then I will like the cows in the picture, notwithstanding cows in pictures are my aversion. I will march up to that picture, with my proud arm about you, & give in my leal & true allegiance without a whimper. Oh, I do it *now*, in fancy. . . .

Don't read a word in that jumping frog book, Livy—*don't*. I hate to hear that infamous volume mentioned. I would be glad to know that every copy of it was burned, & gone forever. I'll never write another like it.

Tell Mr. Langdon he mustn't come in & interrupt you when you are writing to me. It is highly improper, is "such conduct as those." I am both grieved & surprised at it. And he keeps doing it, too—this is the third time. Why this will never do!

Tomorrow will be the New Year, Livy—& the gladdest that ever dawned upon me. The Old Year is passing. Hour by hour, minute by minute, its life ebbs away, & faintly & more faintly its waning pulses beat. I see it, drifting out to join itself to the dead centuries without regret, & yet with many a friendly adieu, with many a grateful parting word for what it has done for me, for what it is doing, for what it is still to do. For it found me a waif, floating at random upon the sea of life, & it leaves me freighted with a good purpose, & blessed with a fair wind, a chart to follow, a port to reach. It found me listless, useless, aimless—it leaves me knighted with noble ambition. It found me well-nigh a skeptic—it leaves me a believer. It found me dead—it leaves me alive. It found me ready to welcome any wind that would blow my vagrant bark abroad, no matter where—it leaves me seeking home & an anchorage, & longing for them. It found me careless of the here & the hereafter—it leaves me with faith in the one & hope for the other. It found my heart scorched, bitter, barren, loveless—& leaves it filled with softening, humanizing, elevating love for the dearest girl on earth, Livy—& I, the homeless then, have on this last day of the dying year, a home that is priceless, a refuge from all the cares & ills of life, in that warm heart of yours, & am supremely happy! And so with grateful benediction I give Godspeed to this good Old Year that is passing away. If I forget all else it has done for me I shall still remember that it gave me your love, Livy, & turned my wandering feet toward the straight gate & the narrow way. Welcome the New Year, with its high resolves, its lofty aspirations! its love, & life, & death! its joy & sorrow! its hidden fates, its awful, curtained mysteries!

Your letter received day before yesterday, I have not even touched upon yet, but still must stop now & go out with the family for the evening. You are a malicious little piece of furniture, Livy, to send me that sketch from the Independent, when you knew perfectly well it would make me cry. *I'll* fix you for it, Miss. But I liked it, you dear good girl, & am glad you sent it. You might have sent me a kiss, too, I should think, these generous Christmas times, you selfish thing.

Now, I *must* stop. Severance was in, a moment ago, & says he will be after me with a buggy promptly at 11 o'clock next year to take me calling—which means *to-morrow.*

Good-bye, Livy, dear—can't take time to read this over & correct it—it wouldn't get in the mail.

Lovingly & *most* lovingly

Sam L. C.

Samuel Clemens and Olivia Langdon were married on the second day of February, 1870, in the Langdon home in Elmira, New York. They would have four children together: three daughters, Susy, Clara, and Jean; and a son, Langdon, who lived only nineteen months. Sam Clemens was a loving and devoted father who truly enjoyed the companionship of his daughters. Susy, the eldest daughter, had a special place in her father's heart, for she aspired to be a writer; but she died tragically at the age of twenty-four. Clara would study the piano and become a professional singer. Jean, the youngest of the Clemens children, was her father's companion and secretary during the last year of his life. Her death, due to complications of epilepsy, occurred just four months before her father's own passing, and Clemens's grief over his daughter caused him to vow never to write again. At left, Olivia Clemens with her three daughters. Photo The Mark Twain House.

HOME IN HARTFORD

FROM *MR. CLEMENS AND MARK TWAIN*, BY JUSTIN KAPLAN

1877

MT delivers an address at a birthday party for John Greenleaf Whittier. The talk, a humorous portrayal of the leading literary figures of the day, is met with silence and hostility by the crowd.

1878

MT and his family begin an extended tour through Europe.

1880

MT begins investing in the Paige typesetter—a machine he hopes will revolutionize the printing industry.

1880

Jean Clemens, MT's youngest child, is born in July.

1881

MT's THE PRINCE AND THE PAUPER is published in December.

1882

MT visits his hometown of Hannibal, Missouri.

1883

MT's LIFE ON THE MISSISSIPPI is published in May.

After their marriage, the Clemenses originally settled in Buffalo, New York, where Sam hoped to make a career as a newspaper man; but neither the work nor the city felt comfortable and the young couple looked instead to Hartford, Connecticut, for a place to make a home and raise their children. The city was a good fit for the young family, and for two decades they lived in a beautiful house on Farmington Avenue on Hartford's west side.

Midway in values as well as distance between New York's commerce and Boston's official culture, Hartford in 1871 was a spacious and pleasant city of about fifty thousand people. It was made prosperous by its booming insurance companies, which had proved their stability once and for all by virtually rebuilding Chicago after the

The Clemenses' extraordinary home, designed by Edward T. Potter and Alfred H. Thorp, was a three-story brick building with nineteen rooms, five balconies, and several gabled roofs. The first floor consisted of the drawing room, the dining room, the kitchen, and the library, which opened into a semi-circular solarium. The first floor also had a guest room and a front hall. On the second level were the family bedrooms as well as a schoolroom for the girls and servants' quarters. The house's third floor was little used by the family, except for the billiard room, in which Clemens did all of his writing while in Hartford. At right, the Hartford house between 1874 and 1881. Photo The Mark Twain House.

great fire, by its silk and leather industries, by the skilled mechanics at its factories and machine shops, by its publishing and printing establishments, and by an appalling output of arms and munitions: peaceable Hartford supplied the Colt revolver, the Sharps rifle, and the Gatling gun to the nation and the world. The poor and the idle were not lacking in the city, though visitors had trouble finding them at first. Soon after he moved to Hartford, Mark Twain was lecturing for the benefit of Father Hawley's strenuous missions to the poor and the alcoholic, and Christmas would find the family sleigh, driven by Patrick McAleer, making the rounds of the needy to deliver baskets which Livy had loaded with turkeys, oranges, canned peas, raisins, and nuts. But despite these challenges to the social conscience the fact

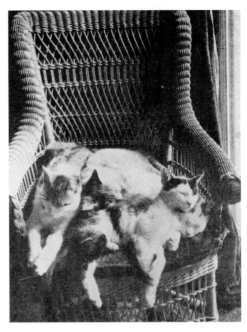

The house on Farmington Avenue was full of life— not only the Clemenses, their children, and their continual flow of guests, but also animals, particularly cats and dogs. Above, some of the Clemenses' cats. Photo the Chemung County Historical Society, Elmira, NY.

The Clemenses maintained an extravagant lifestyle in Hartford. They entertained almost nightly while in residence and employed a full staff. They also poured a small fortune into renovations, most significantly a major redecoration performed by the firm of Louis Comfort Tiffany and Associated Artists in 1880–1881. At left, the family library. Photo The Mark Twain House.

remained that Hartford, if its wealth were averaged among its citizens, was the most affluent of American cities.

What brought Mark Twain to Hartford was not its downtown but a small settlement on what was then the western extremity of the city. Twenty years earlier the lawyer John Hooker, husband of the formidable Isabella Beecher and descendant of Thomas Hooker, who had led a march from Cambridge Common in 1636 and founded Hartford, bought a one-hundred acre tract of wooded land known as Nook Farm. John Hooker was a sagacious real-estate developer; he was also careful in choosing his neighbors. As he sold off the land parcel by parcel and saw ample and gracious houses going up among the trees, he had the double reward of reaping a profit on his investment and of building a community of relatives and closely linked friends. Hooker's distinguished brother-in-law, Francis Gillette, United States Senator, abolitionist, and temperance reformer, built and lived at Nook Farm. Gillette's son, William, encouraged by Mark Twain, moved on to an acting career capped by the role of Sherlock Holmes; the Senator's daughter, Lilly, married George Warner and lived at Nook Farm. So did Isabella's sisters Mary, with her husband Thomas Perkins, a lawyer, and Harriet, with her husband Calvin Stowe, educator and Bible exegete and in appearance something of an eccentric: Professor Stowe's nose, ravaged by a disease, was like a cauliflower, his long white beard hung down on his chest, and, Clemens recalled, he looked like Santa Claus on the loose. Among others at Nook Farm were the co-editors of The Hartford *Courant*: Joseph Hawley, major general of volunteers during the war, and after it governor of Connecticut, Congressman, and Senator; and George Warner's brother, Charles Dudley Warner, Mark Twain's next-door neighbor and his collaborator on *The Gilded Age*. Nook Farm was as staunchly committed to liberal Congregationalism as it was to the Republican party. In 1864 the group had raised most of the $100,000 it would eventually cost to build the Asylum Hill Congregational Church, a spired edifice of Portland stone a few blocks away from the property limits of Nook Farm. Mark Twain called it "the Church of the Holy Speculators." Its minister was his friend Joseph Twichell.

In the fall of 1871, when Clemens rented the Hooker house on Forest Street, where he had once been a guest, and moved in with Livy, who was pregnant again, the white-faced and sickly infant Langdon, and their coachman, cook, and housemaid, he was at the pleasant and enveloping center of the Beecher network. A few years later, when the Beecher scandal was playing to a national audience from the center ring, the threads began to ravel. At the moment, though, for Livy, whose closest friend was Isabella's daughter, Alice Day, and even for Clemens, who had reached something of an accommodation with Isabella, the Hooker-Beecher world was home, welcoming, and so familiar that soon after they were settled on Forest Street Livy said, "You'd know this house was built by a Beecher. It's so queer."

Clemens achieved a remarkable degree of community and identification with his Nook Farm neighbors. For the first time since his boyhood in Hannibal he was part of the fabric of a stable society, and although he turned a bitter eye on practically every American phenomenon of his time he rarely questioned his life in Hartford. Nook Farm was an enclave walled off from a demoralized nation. He shared the group's faith in a dynamic aristocracy, their high responsibility, their earnest idealism, and their intellectual dedication. Harriet Beecher Stowe and Charles Dudley Warner were among the few American authors who made from their work a living comparable to that of a modest merchant prince, and they welcomed Mark Twain all the more warmly because he shared their sense of professionalism in writing and showed promise of becoming the most successful practitioner of them all.

Clemens also shared their gregariousness, their taste for entertaining each other and any eminence who happened to be passing through Hartford. . . . Visitors to Nook Farm like William Dean Howells were overwhelmed by the boundless fellowship and informality. The Warners and the Clemenses, Howells wrote to a friend in Ohio, "live very near each other, in a sort of suburban grove, and their neighbors are the Stowes and the Hookers, and a great many delightful people. They go in and out of each other's houses without ringing, and nobody gets more than the first syllable of his first name—they call their minister *Joe* Twichell." The price of all this sociability, which was supplemented by teas and musicales, by billiards, discussion groups, and whist drives, was high, in energy as well as money. Mark Twain the professional writer could work full time only during the three or four summer months he spent away from Hartford in the relative isolation of his sister-in-law's farm above Elmira. The rest of the year he thought of as enforced vacation. The Nook Farm residents tended to build as well as entertain on a scale beyond their incomes. They were always, symbolically at least, a little overdrawn at the bank. Mark Twain carried their cautious prodigality to a dimension of spectacular opulence unknown to American writers before him. When he built his own house there, that eccentric, willful, and eye-catching whatnot, $70,000 worth of turrets and balconies housing $21,000 worth of furniture and perched on a five-acre $31,000 tract of land, Nook Farm received from its newest member its gaudiest landmark, and eventually, instead of merely going into debt, Clemens went into bankruptcy.

During his Hartford years, Clemens completed the books upon which his reputation was built: THE GILDED AGE, THE ADVENTURES OF TOM SAWYER, A TRAMP ABROAD, THE PRINCE AND THE PAUPER, LIFE ON THE MISSISSIPPI, ADVENTURES OF HUCKLEBERRY FINN, *and* A CONNECTICUT YANKEE IN KING ARTHUR'S COURT. *Above, an interior view of the Farmington Avenue residence. Photo The Mark Twain House.*

The pleasantest view I had of the city was from the cozy fireside in that wonderful home of Mr. S. L. Clemens, who was my host during my stay in Hartford. . . . I think I have never been in a home more beautifully homelike than this palace of the king of humorists. The surroundings of the house are beautiful, and its quaint architecture, broad East Indian porticos, the Greek patterns in mosaic in the dark red brick walls attract and charm the attention and good taste of the passer-by, for the home, inside and out, is the perfection of exquisite taste and harmony. But with all its architectural beauty and originality, the elegance of its interior finish and decorations, the greatest charm about the house is the atmosphere of "homelikeness" that pervades it. Charmingly as he can entertain thousands of people at a time from the platform, Mr. Clemens is even a more perfect entertainer in his home. The brightest and best sides of his nature shine out at his fireside. The humor and drollery that sparkle in his conversation are as utterly unaffected and natural as sunlight. Indeed, I don't believe he knows or thinks that most of his talk before the sparkling fire, up in the pleasant retirement of his billiard room study, is marketable merchandise worth so much a page to the publishers, but it is. And it is not all drollery and humor. He is so earnest that his earnestness charms you fully as much as his brightest flashes, and once in a while there is in his voice an inflection of wonderful pathos, so touched with melancholy that you look into the kind earnest eyes to see what thought has touched his voice. And he has a heart as big as his body; I believe there does not live a man more thoroughly unselfish and self-forgetful. . . .

Mr. R. J. Burdette, from a letter to the Burlington, Iowa HAWKEYE, *1880*

FROM *THE ADVENTURES OF TOM SAWYER*

BY MARK TWAIN

1889

MT's A CONNECTICUT YANKEE IN KING ARTHUR'S COURT *is published in December.*

1890

Jane Lampton Clemens, MT's mother, dies on October 27.

Perhaps no scene from the fiction of Mark Twain is as familiar and celebrated as the fence painting incident from the second chapter of THE ADVENTURES OF TOM SAWYER. *The scene is commemorated each year in Hannibal with a fence painting competition during Tom Sawyer Days. Clemens admitted to inventing the scene while visiting England in the early 1870s. Below, artist J.G. Brown illustrates Tom's creative solution to the hard work of fence painting. Illustration The Mark Twain House.*

THE ADVENTURES OF TOM SAWYER *is the story of one summer in the life of a young boy in Missouri at the beginning of the nineteenth century. In some senses, it is quite autobiographical—the people, places, and times are much as Clemens knew them as a boy in Hannibal. But the book is also full of dramatic embellishment and creative invention. It is a combination that has proven timeless. First published in 1876, the book, promoted as a book for boys, is the best selling of all the works of Mark Twain. It has never been out of print since its first edition and has appeared in as many as three dozen languages. For Americans in particular, Tom Sawyer's story recalls a time—whether real or purely the invention of a nostalgic memory—when summer was endless, boys were innocent, and life was simple.*

But Tom's energy did not last. He began to think of the fun he had planned for this day, and his sorrows multiplied. Soon the free boys would come tripping along on all sorts of delicious expeditions, and they would make a world of fun of him for having to work—the very thought of it burnt him like fire. He got out his worldly wealth and examined it—bits of toys, marbles, and trash; enough to buy an exchange of *work*, maybe, but not half enough to buy so much as a half an hour of pure freedom. So he returned his straitened means to his pocket and gave up the idea of trying to buy the boys. At this dark and hopeless moment an inspiration burst upon him! Nothing less than a great, magnificent inspiration.

He took up his brush and went tranquilly to work. Ben Rogers hove in sight presently—the very boy, of all boys, whose ridicule he had been dreading. Ben's gait was the hop-skip-and-jump—proof enough that his heart was light and his anticipations high. He was eating an apple, and giving a long, melodious whoop, at intervals, followed by a deep-toned ding-dong-dong, ding-dong-dong, for he was personating a steamboat. As he drew near, he slackened speed, took the middle of the street, leaned far over to starboard and rounded to ponderously and with laborious pomp and circumstance—for he was personating the *Big Missouri*, and considered himself to be drawing nine feet of water. He was boat and captain and engine bells combined, so he had to imagine himself standing on his own hurricane deck giving the orders and executing them. . . .

Tom went on whitewashing—paid no attention to the steamboat. Ben stared a moment and then said:

"Hi-*yi*! *You're* up a stump, ain't you!"

No answer. Tom surveyed his last touch with the eye of an artist, then he gave his brush another gentle sweep and surveyed the result, as before. Ben ranged up alongside of him. Tom's mouth watered for the apple, but he stuck to his work. Ben said:

"Hello, old chap, you got to work, hey?"

Tom wheeled suddenly and said:

"Why it's you, Ben! I warn't noticing."

"*Say—I*'m going in a-swimming, *I* am. Don't you wish you could? But of course you'd druther *work*—wouldn't you? Course you would!"

Tom contemplated the boy a bit, and said:

"What do you call work?"

"Why, ain't *that* work?"

Tom resumed his whitewashing, and answered carelessly:

"Well, maybe it is, and maybe it ain't. All I know is, it suits Tom Sawyer."

"Oh, come, now, you don't mean to let on that you *like* it?"

The brush continued to move.

"Like it? Well, I don't see why I oughtn't to like it. Does a boy get a chance to whitewash a fence every day?"

That put the thing in a new light. Ben stopped nibbling his apple. Tom swept his brush daintily back and forth—stepped back to note the effect—added a touch here and there—criticized the effect again—Ben watching every move and getting more and more interested, more and more absorbed. Presently, he said:

"Say, Tom, let *me* whitewash a little."

Tom considered, was about to consent; but he altered his mind:

"No—no—I reckon it wouldn't hardly do, Ben. You see, Aunt Polly's awful particular about this fence—right here on the street, you know—but if it was the back fence I wouldn't mind and *she* wouldn't. Yes, she's awful particular about this fence; it's got to be done very careful; I reckon there ain't one boy in a thousand, maybe two thousand that can do it the way it's got to be done."

"No—is that so? Oh, come now—lemme just try. Only just a little—I'd let *you*, if you was me, Tom."

"Ben, I'd like to, honest Injun, but Aunt Polly—well, Jim wanted to do it, but she wouldn't let him; Sid wanted to do it, and she wouldn't let Sid. Now don't you see how I'm fixed? If you was to tackle this fence and anything was to happen to it—"

"Oh, shucks, I'll be just as careful. Now lemme try. Say—I'll give you the core of my apple."

"Well, here— No, Ben, now don't. I'm afeared—"

"I'll give you *all* of it!"

Tom gave up his brush with reluctance in his face, but alacrity in his heart. And while the late steamer *Big Missouri* worked and sweated in the sun, the retired artist sat on a barrel in the shade close by, dangled his legs, munched his apple, and planned the slaughter of more innocents. . . .

When the copyright on The Adventures of Tom Sawyer *expired in 1931, a handful of new editions of the novel appeared, most notably a 1936 edition featuring the illustrations of Norman Rockwell. Rockwell would also complete illustrations for* Adventures of Huckleberry Finn. *His images pair perfectly with Twain's prose and bring even more vividly to life the characters and scenes already so colorful and real on the page. Above, Rockwell's fence painting scene from* The Adventures of Tom Sawyer.

THE FATHER OF THREE LITTLE GIRLS

FROM *MY FATHER: MARK TWAIN,* BY CLARA CLEMENS

In 1931, Clara Clemens published MY FATHER: MARK TWAIN, *a biography of her father. The book is an affectionate memoir that has proven to be an invaluable resource for students and biographers looking for firsthand information about Clemens's life, particularly his final decades.*

Below, an artist's depiction of Samuel Clemens and his two oldest daughters, Susy and Clara. The author was devoted to his three girls, but, sadly, only Clara would outlive him and give him a grandchild. Photo The Mark Twain House.

Father never showed the least sign of being bored when my sister Susy and I clambered upon his knee begging for a "long" story. This entertainment usually took place in the room we called the library, which was our living-room. In the large fireplace great logs blazed almost continuously, for in spite of furnace heat this room was often cold, owing to winds that howled about the windows during the winter season. The library as well as the dining-room faced a small river and wooded ravine. Seated in a large armchair in front of the fire, with my sister and me in his lap, Father would start a story about the pictures on the wall. Passing from picture to picture, his power of invention led us into countries and among human figures that held us spellbound. He treated a Medusa head according to his own individual method, the snakes being sometimes changed to laurel leaves that tickled joy in Medusa's hair and inspired thoughts of victory. If the colored butler, George, interrupted the tale by announcing a caller, or a meal ready to be served, our hearts sank and did not rise until Father returned to the tales of the pictures. He must have had unflinching patience and I have sometimes wondered if my mother did not send in the butler on imaginary errands to protect him against too much discomfort from the insatiable demands of his tiny auditors.

There was a beautiful conservatory off the library and the scent from the plants brought reality to some of the tropical scenes described by Father. One day a snake came wriggling into the room across the rugs straight for our chair. He must have gotten in from the conservatory but how he found his way there we never guessed. Father dropped us both to the floor and seizing a pair of tongs from the fireplace lifted the snake in the air and precipitated him through a door in the bay window that faced the wooded ravine. This incident relieved Father from any further oratory that afternoon.

There was something romantic, even dramatic, about the atmosphere of this home of ours in Hartford, Connecticut. It was a brick building with many little turrets, porches, and towers. Three floors of various-shaped rooms provided suitable scenes for almost any novel or drama one might be reading. There was a guest-room on the third floor next father's study and billiard-room. This room was so spooky that my sisters and I decided it was a suitable home for the insane wife of Rochester in *Jane Eyre*. On this floor, too, in a small gabled room where I kept some rather wild squirrels, we imprisoned a sea pirate to whom we passed meager food through a gridiron nailed on the door until the cook instituted a thorough search for the missing utensil, which was required for the cooking of chops. After this the pirate was allowed to die and his place was filled by St. Francis, who, we hoped, would tame the squirrels.

Father was always ready to make jokes at the breakfast table, and my impression is that his wit was not half appreciated at that hour of the morning. Everybody was present in the dining-room by eight o'clock, but I don't think anyone wished to be. I would say that my father was the only one at the table who found any real joy in life so early in the morning, and of course he didn't *find* it; he created it.

As I think back on the years I spent in his company, I realize that there was rarely an hour when something of his genius did not shine forth. Even when surrounded by comforts and luxuries, he never sank into their clutches. He did not become "comfortable" to the detriment of his intellect and soul. Both were continually on fire. Not even in sleep could I imagine his mind completely at rest. Wherever he was, he created a world of energized thought. The force in his personality, resulting from an ever-productive brain and a Latin temperament, electrified some people to a certain false brilliancy which only belonged to them in his presence. Those who were habitually stupid became intelligent, and those who were brilliant became super-brilliant. Sparks started by Father grew to flames in their passage from brain to brain. Although a very small child, when guests like Nansen, the explorer, Sir Edwin Arnold, or eminent actors, Edwin Booth and Henry Irving among them, graced our hearthstone, I remember feeling that the dynamic figure of Mark Twain did not pale by their side.

In spite of a very full life, my father found time for his three little girls, and thought of many ways to amuse them. After a visit to Montreal, where he and my mother were entertained by the Viceroy, he returned with not only the gayest-colored toboggan costumes for my sisters and me, but a full-sized toboggan. At the same time he supplied us with three collies that we christened "I know," "You know," and "Don't know."

A toboggan slide had to be arranged behind the house, but this was not difficult, as our home stood on the top of a small hill that sloped gradually to a rather broad meadow bounded on the far side by a river. Father was as jubilant as any of us the first day we gathered on the crest of the hill to try the new toboggan. Viewed from the street at a distance of forty yards, we must have formed a bright picture on that sparkling winter's day—three small girls in their blue, yellow, and red costumes surrounded by three gamboling dogs, directed by a picturesque man dressed in a sealskin coat with a cap drawn down over his curly gray hair. The dogs barked so loudly, and the children laughed so much, that I doubt whether Father's explanations of the art of tobogganing were much appreciated.

In any case, either on that day or a few days later, we had a serious accident. Flying down the hill at full speed, the toboggan was hurled by some obstacle into a great oak tree. I was the only one hurt, but my damages were severe. One leg was bent around into the shape of a half-moon, and after the gardener and coachman had carried me into the house, my shoe had to be cut off the crooked foot.

Father and Mother were giving a large dinner party that night and it was too late to call it off. So at intervals during the meal they took turns paying me brief calls, while the physician did his utmost to relieve their anxiety. The next day it appeared likely that my leg would have to be amputated. But this misfortune, through care and skill, was prevented.

Langdon was Sam and Livy Clemens's firstborn child and their only son. Born prematurely, he was a sickly child whose development was so delayed that he never walked in his nineteen months of life. His brief life ended in June of 1872. The official cause was diphtheria, but Clemens, who had taken Langdon out for a ride in the carriage and allowed his blanket to fall off, always blamed himself for his son's death. Above, Langdon Clemens. Photo The Mark Twain House.

During this period I slept in my parents' bedroom in a large Dutch bed that had an angel on each of the four posts. Since earliest infancy my sisters and I had always adored this bed. The angels could be removed and we frequently took them down and washed them in a small bathtub. Doubtless my mother thought it would be easier for me to endure the pain from my twisted leg if I could be near the four angels night and day.

Father was so upset over the accident that he was constantly concerned with schemes to cheer me up and help the time to pass. Among other pleasant surprises, he arranged to have one hundred valentines sent to me on St. Valentine's Day. It was one of the biggest events of my entire childhood, for I had always loved pictures, and here they were showered upon me so fast that hardly had I finished exclaiming over the bright colors of one before another dropped into my lap!

SUMMERS AT WORK

FROM *MY FATHER: MARK TWAIN*, BY CLARA CLEMENS

The Clemenses' home in Hartford was part of Nook Farm, a 140-acre community along the banks of the Park River in Hartford. The community was begun by John Hooker and his brother-in-law in 1853. The Clemenses found their way to Nook Farm through Isabella Beecher Hooker, who was a close friend of Livy's mother and the wife of the community's founder. Mrs. Hooker was also a prominent suffragist and a leader in the fight for women's rights. Isabella's sister, Harriet Beecher Stowe, was also a Nook Farm resident. Above, Clemens, Livy, and their three daughters on the porch of their Hartford home. Photo The Mark Twain Papers.

Quarry Farm was the home of Clemens's sister-in-law, Susan Langdon Crane, and her family. Between 1871 and 1889, the Clemenses spent most of their summer months at the farm, where Clemens had a private octagonal study in a secluded spot. It was here, and not in the ever-bustling house in Hartford, that he found the solitude to write.

The major part of Father's work was accomplished in the summer, which we spent with my mother's sister, Mrs. Theodore Crane. She lived on the top of a long hill overlooking Elmira, New York. The place was called Quarry Farm, and was a heavenly spot. On a sunny day one could see the Chemung River sparkling far below as it wound its way through the town of Elmira, nestled cozily between the hills surrounding it. At night the streets and houses, though at a great distance, seemed ablaze with artificial fire. It was a lovely sight.

The house in which my aunt lived was simple but very comfortable, with enough rooms to accommodate our family. Susy and I slept together, my younger sister, Jean, roomed with the nurse, and Father and Mother occupied a third room. Mrs. Crane often referred to her home as "Do as you Please Hall," for she wished everyone to feel complete liberty to act and think as he would. Her own nature was so sweet and gentle that one could not imagine a more suitable abode for her than this picturesque and peaceful farm elevated above the plane of ordinary mortals. She was as tranquil and lovable as the trees and flowers, her most constant companions.

Aunt Sue, for whom my elder sister was named, was the one person I have ever seen who appeared to be continually above and beyond the hurts inflicted by human existence. Father sometimes called her Saint Sue, and she returned the compliment by baptizing him Holy Samuel, though with a strong touch of humor in her tone of voice whenever she used this title. Aunt Sue adored Father's little bursts of temper and would laugh at him most heartily. Often he laughed with her, altering his vehement mood instantaneously to one of childlike mirth. These sudden changes from shadow to light, and from light to shadow, were perhaps one of Father's real charms, for the human race likes surprises.

There was a small rise of ground at the summit of the main hill, stretching off to one side like an extra branch to a tree. Halfway up this elevation stood the little octagonal cottage in which father did all his writing. One reached it by a winding path and about twenty stone steps. It was a charming sort of Peter Pan house covered with ivy and surrounded by beautiful wild flowers and morning-glories. Through the tops of the trees an aperture had been made so that Father could enjoy the view of Elmira and the hills beyond—an inspiring place for creative work. In spite of the eight good-sized windows, the air was so permeated with tobacco smoke that it was almost stifling to one unused to it. Father seemed to thrive on it, notwithstanding, and in fact, the less he followed the good advice of physicians the better he seemed to feel. No exercise, little fresh air, constant inhaling of cigar smoke—all contributed to keep him in good health.

Once settled at the farm for the summer, he had no desire to leave it even for a short visit to town. He was devoted to some of Mother's friends and relatives there, but he very much preferred their coming to see him on the hill than calling on them in the valley. There was a fascination about the peace of the place that worked like a spell. Usually he went to his study about ten o'clock in the morning and remained until five in the afternoon, seldom taking anything to eat or drink in the middle of the day.

We dined at six o'clock, and the evening was spent in various ways. Often Father read aloud to the whole family the work he had accomplished during the day. Again, he and Theodore Crane, his brother-in-law, played games, either chess or cards, while Mother read aloud to the rest of us. No matter how engrossed Father might appear to be in the game he was playing, he managed to hear enough of the reading to throw out very humorous criticisms of the author's style, particularly if the author happened to be Meredith (whom he thought too wordy) or Jane Austen, a pet aversion of his.

Sometimes immediately after dinner, while there was still daylight, we strolled into a large field near by for a strange purpose. A plan had been laid for building a stone tower, at the top of which Father could muse, forgetting the world. Each member of the family was to compete with the others in gathering the greatest number of stones to be used in erecting the tower. I think that Father represented the bottom and I the top of the class in this undertaking. He would pick up a stone, and become so interested in the imprint left in the ground where it had lain or in the shape of the stone itself, that his tongue flowed with observations while his feet stood still. I doubt if he added more than a dozen stones to the pile during one whole summer, and the tower was never built.

The Clemenses, like most other wealthy Hartford families of their day, were in the habit of leaving the city during the summertime, which could be rather hot and humid in central Connecticut. Sam and Livy and their girls spent the summer of 1890 in New York's Catskill Mountains at Onteora Park, a summer retreat for artists, writers, and their families. Most summers, however, were spent in Elmira, Livy's native city, at Quarry Farm, the residence of Livy's sister. Today, the city of Elmira is home to the Center for Mark Twain Studies. Below, Clemens and daughter Susy play parts in a humorous production of Hero and Leander *at the Onteora Club. Photo The Mark Twain House.*

FROM *LIFE ON THE MISSISSIPPI*

BY MARK TWAIN

In 1874, Clemens wrote a series of articles for his friend William Dean Howells's ATLANTIC MONTHLY *magazine. The articles, under the title "Old Times on the Mississippi," were a memoir of his piloting days. Eventually, they became the basis for chapters four through seventeen of the novel* LIFE ON THE MISSISSIPPI. *Illustration by Edmund C. Garrett from* LIFE ON THE MISSISSIPPI, *The Mark Twain House.*

LIFE ON THE MISSISSIPPI *combines reminiscences about Clemens's steamboat pilot days and his childhood on the river with insights and information gathered during a return visit to the river in 1882. Like most of the work of Mark Twain,* LIFE ON THE MISSISSIPPI *is a blend of biography and invention. Clemens was always fond of the book, which he felt was important as a document of a significant era in American history. Here, he speaks of the ardors of learning to navigate the river as a steamboat pilot.*

Now when I had mastered the language of this water, and had come to know every trifling feature that bordered the great river as familiarly as I knew the letters of the alphabet, I had made a valuable acquisition. But I had lost something, too. I had lost something which could never be restored to me while I lived. All the grace, the beauty, the poetry, had gone out of the majestic river! I still kept in mind a certain wonderful sunset which I witnessed when steamboating was new to me. A broad expanse of the river was turned to blood; in the middle distance the red hue brightened into gold, through which a solitary log came floating, black and conspicuous; in one place a long, slanting mark lay sparkling upon the water; in another the surface was broken by boiling, tumbling rings, that were as many-tinted as an opal; where the ruddy flush was faintest, was a smooth spot that was covered with graceful circles and radiating lines, ever so delicately traced; the shore on our left was densely wooded, and the somber shadow that fell from this forest was broken in one place by a long, ruffled trail that shone like silver; and high above the forest wall a clean-stemmed dead tree waved a single leafy bough that glowed like a flame in the unobstructed splendor that was flowing from the sun. There were graceful curves, reflected images, woody heights, soft distances; and over the whole scene, far and near, the dissolving lights drifted steadily, enriching it every passing moment with new marvels of coloring.

I stood like one bewitched. I drank it in, in a speechless rapture. The world was new to me, and I had never seen anything like this at home. But as I have said, a day came when I began to cease from noting the glories and the charms which the moon and the sun and the twilight wrought upon the river's face; another day came when I ceased altogether to note them. Then, if that sunset scene had been repeated, I should have looked upon it without rapture, and should have commented upon it, inwardly, after this fashion: "This sun means that we are going to have wind to-morrow; that floating log means that the river is rising, small thanks to it; that slanting mark on the water refers to a bluff reef which is going to kill somebody's steamboat one of these nights, if it keeps on stretching out like that; those tumbling 'boils' show a dissolving bar and a changing channel there; the lines and circles in the slick water over yonder are a warning that that troublesome place is shoaling up dangerously; that silver streak in the shadow of the forest is the 'break' from a new snag, and he has located himself in the very best place he could have found to fish for steamboats; that tall dead tree, with a single living branch, is not going to last long, and then how is a body ever going to get through this blind place at night without the friendly old landmark?"

No, the romance and beauty were all gone from the river. All the value any feature of it had for me now was the amount of usefulness it could furnish toward compassing the safe piloting of a steamboat. Since those days, I have pitied doctors from my heart. What does the lovely flush in a beauty's cheek mean to a doctor but a "break" that ripples above some deadly disease? Are not all her visible charms sown thick with what are to him the signs and symbols of hidden decay? Does he ever see her beauty at all, or doesn't he simply view her professionally, and comment upon her unwholesome condition all to himself? And doesn't he sometimes wonder whether he has gained most or lost most by learning his trade?

THE LECTURE FIELD

FROM *THE AUTOBIOGRAPHY OF MARK TWAIN*, EDITED BY CHARLES NEIDER

Clemens's career as a writer and speaker paralleled the height of a lecture craze in the United States. In the years after the Civil War, audiences across the country clamored for speakers to entertain, enlighten, and educate them. In 1884, Clemens toured with George Washington Cable, a Southern writer. Billed as the "twins of genius," the two combined humor, singing, and readings from their works on a hundred-city tour. The tour was a smashing success, but the long months on the road together put an end to the friendship between the two men. Clemens describes the experience in this excerpt from his autobiography.

Cable had been scouting the country alone for three years with readings from his novels and he had been a good reader in the beginning, for he had been born with a natural talent for it, but unhappily he prepared himself for his public work by taking lessons from a teacher of elocution, and so by the time he was ready to begin his platform work he was so well and thoroughly educated that he was merely theatrical and artificial and not half as pleasing and entertaining to a house as he had been in the splendid days of his ignorance. I had never tried reading as a trade and I wanted to try it. . . .

It was ghastly! At least in the beginning. I had selected my readings well enough but had not studied them. I supposed it would only be necessary to do like Dickens—get out on the platform and read from the book. I did that and made a botch of it. Written things are not for speech; their form is literary; they are stiff, inflexible and will not lend themselves to happy and effective delivery with the tongue—where their purpose is to merely entertain, not instruct; they have to be limbered up, broken up, colloquialized and turned into the common forms of unpremeditated talk—otherwise they will bore the house, not entertain it. After a week's experience with the book I laid it aside and never carried it to the platform again; but meantime I had memorized those pieces, and in delivering them from the platform they soon transformed themselves into flexible talk, with all their obstructing precisenesses and formalities gone out of them for good. . . .

Clemens, pictured above in 1875, gave more than one thousand lectures during a career that spanned nearly thirty years. He loved being the center of attention, loved the laughter and appreciation of the crowd, but hated the traveling and repetition. Most often, he would return to lecturing only to bolster his fluctuating finances. Photo The Mark Twain House.

FROM *ADVENTURES OF HUCKLEBERRY FINN*

BY MARK TWAIN

By the time Mark Twain's ADVENTURES OF HUCKLEBERRY FINN *appeared in print in America in 1885, it had been eight long years in the writing and had undergone a transformation from its original conception as a sequel to* TOM SAWYER. HUCK FINN *is, like* THE ADVENTURES OF TOM SAWYER, *a humorous story of boyhood, but it is also much that the previous novel most definitely is not.* HUCK FINN *is a book with profound and powerful themes, a book that openly examines issues of racism and morality, a book that broke new ground in American fiction by using as a narrator a young boy who spoke in a true American vernacular. Modern critics rate* HUCK FINN *among the classics of American literature; and, although not the largest selling of Mark Twain's novels, it is surely the most studied and the most debated. Below, E. W. Kemble's cover illustration from the first edition of* ADVENTURES OF HUCKLEBERRY FINN, *The Mark Twain House.*

The voice of Huck Finn telling his own story is unquestionably the great strength of ADVENTURES OF HUCKLEBERRY FINN. *To some nineteenth-century readers, however, accustomed as they were to omniscient and refined narrative voices, Huck's coarse language rendered the book not only offensive, but dangerous as an influence on young minds. Such readers led the charge to ban the book from public library shelves; they succeeded only in providing the author with some free publicity. The book's language—colorful, rough, and truly authentic to its time and place—has remained at the center of controversy for more than one hundred years, and the novel's value is questioned whenever readers fail to grasp the distance between the simple, uneducated boy who tells the story and the author who created him.*

Once I said to myself it would be a thousand times better for Jim to be a slave at home where his family was, as long as he'd *got* to be a slave, and so I'd better write a letter to Tom Sawyer and tell him to tell Miss Watson where he was. But I soon give up that notion for two things: she'd be mad and disgusted at his rascality and ungratefulness for leaving her, and so she'd sell him straight down the river again; and if she didn't, everybody naturally despises an ungrateful nigger, and they'd make Jim feel it all the time, and so he'd feel ornery and disgraced. And then think of *me!* It would get all around that Huck Finn helped a nigger to get his freedom; and if I was ever to see anybody from that town again I'd be ready to get down and lick his boots for shame. That's just the way: a person does a low-down thing, and then he don't want to take no consequences of it. Thinks as long as he can hide, it ain't no disgrace. That was my fix exactly. The more I studied about this the more my conscience went to grinding me, and the more wicked and low-down and ornery I got to feeling. And at last, when it hit me all of a sudden that here was the plain hand of Providence slapping me in the face and letting me know my wickedness was being watched all the time from up there in heaven, whilst I was stealing a poor old woman's nigger that hadn't ever done me no harm, and now was showing me there's One that's always on the lookout, and ain't a-going to allow no such miserable doings to go only just so fur and no further, I most dropped in my tracks I was so scared. Well, I tried the best I could to kinder soften it up somehow for myself by saying I was brung up wicked, and so I warn't so much to blame; but something inside me kept saying, "There was the Sunday-school, you could 'a' gone to it; and if you'd 'a' done it they'd 'a' learnt you there that people that acts as I'd been acting about that nigger goes to everlasting fire."

It made me shiver. And I about made up my mind to pray, and see if I couldn't try to quit being the kind of a boy I was and be better. So I kneeled down. But the words wouldn't come. Why wouldn't they? It warn't no use to try and hide it from Him. Nor from *me,* neither. I knowed very well why they wouldn't come. It was because my heart warn't right; it was because I warn't square; it was because I was playing double. I was letting *on* to give up sin, but away inside of me I was holding on to the biggest one of all. I was trying to make my mouth *say* I would do the right thing and the clean thing, and go and write to that nigger's owner and tell where he was; but deep down in me I knowed it was a lie, and He knowed it. You can't pray a lie—I found that out.

So I was full of trouble, full as I could be; and didn't know what to do. At last I had an idea; and I says, I'll go and write that letter—and *then* see if I can pray. Why, it was astonishing, the way I felt as light as a feather right straight off, and my troubles all gone. So I got a piece of paper and a pencil, all glad and excited, and set down and wrote:

> *Miss Watson, your runaway nigger Jim is down here two mile below Pikesville, and*
> *Mr. Phelps has got him and he will give him up for the reward if you send.*
>
> HUCK FINN.

I felt good and all washed clean of sin for the first time I had ever felt so in my life, and I knowed I could pray now. But I didn't do it straight off, but laid the paper down and set there thinking—thinking how good it was all this happened so, and how near I come to being lost and going to hell. And went on thinking. And got to thinking over our trip down the river; and I see Jim before me all time: in the day and in the night-time, sometimes moonlight, sometimes storms, and we a-floating along, talking and singing and laughing. But somehow I couldn't seem to strike no places to harden me against him, but only the other kind. I'd see him standing my watch on top of his'n, 'stead of calling me, so I could go on sleeping; and see him how glad he was when I come back out of the fog; and when I come to him again in the swamp, up there where the feud was; and such-like times; and would always call me honey, and pet me, and do everything he could think of for me, and how good he always was; and at last I struck the time I saved him by telling the men we had smallpox aboard, and he was so grateful, and said I was the best friend old Jim ever had in the world, and the *only* one he's got now; and then I happened to look around and see that paper.

It was a close place. I took it up, and held it in my hand. I was a-trembling, because I'd got to decide, forever, betwixt two things, and I knowed it. I studied a minute, sort of holding my breath, and then says to myself:

"All right, then, I'll *go* to hell!"—and tore it up.

It was awful thoughts and awful words, but they was said. And I let them stay said; and never thought no more about reforming. I shoved the whole thing out of my head, and said I would take up wickedness again, which was in my line, being brung up to it, and the other warn't. And for a starter I would go to work and steal Jim out of slavery again; and if I could think up anything worse, I would do that, too; because as long as I was in, and in for good, I might as well go the whole hog. . . .

In his latest story, HUCKLEBERRY FINN . . . by Mark Twain, Mr. Clemens has made a very distinct literary advance over TOM SAWYER, as an interpreter of human nature and a contributor to our stock of original pictures of American life. Still adhering to his plan of narrating the adventures of boys, with a primeval and Robin Hood freshness, he has broadened his canvas and given us a picture of a people, of a geographical region, of a life that is new in the world. The scene of his romance is the Mississippi River. Mr. Clemens has written of this river before specifically, but he has not before presented it to the imagination so distinctly nor so powerfully. Huck Finn's voyage down the Mississippi with the runaway nigger Jim, and with occasionally other companions, is an adventure fascinating in itself as any of the classic outlaw stories, but in order that the reader may know what the author has done for him, let him notice the impression left on his mind of this lawless, mysterious, wonderful Mississippi, when he has closed the book. But it is not alone the river that is indelibly impressed upon the mind, the life that went up and down it and went on along its banks is projected with extraordinary power. Incidentally, and with a true artistic instinct, the villages, the cabins, the people of this river become startlingly real. The beauty of this is that it is apparently done without effort. Huck floating down the river happens to see these things and to encounter the people and the characters that made the river famous forty years ago—that is all. They do not have the air of being invented, but of being found. And the dialects of the people, white and black—what a study are they; and yet nobody talks for the sake of exhibiting a dialect. It is not necessary to believe the surprising adventures that Huck engages in, but no one will have a moment's doubt of the reality of the country and the people he meets. . . .

from THE HARTFORD COURANT, February 20, 1885

A Generous Action

FROM *THE HARTFORD COURANT*, APRIL 1885

The Committee of the Public Library of Concord, Mass., have unanimously voted to exclude from their shelves Mark Twain's latest book, HUCKLEBERRY FINN. *We are glad to see that the commendation given to this sort of literature by its publication in the* CENTURY *has received a check by this action at Concord.*

THE BOSTON LITERARY WORLD, *March 21, 1885*

Clemens responded to the controversy over ADVENTURES OF HUCKLEBERRY FINN *with humor, sarcasm, and a sound understanding that the end result of the much-discussed banning of his book would be free publicity and an increase in audience. In this April 1885 article in* THE HARTFORD COURANT, *Clemens addresses his detractors and admirers in the state of Massachusetts after the Concord Public Library issues its ban on* HUCKLEBERRY FINN.

Indeed, some of the leading newspapers of the country have taken the liberty to laugh at the Concord folks for their conduct, and the libraries that have rejected the volume are, we venture to say, few and far between. They must all be of the class that the Concord library belongs to; for one of the trustees of that library, when interviewed on the matter, said that no fiction was permitted on the Concord shelves. Of course, "Huckleberry Finn" isn't a true story. It is fiction, and so it's barred by this Concord limitation. The discovery that they had bought a biography in good faith and had got something that was not true may be the cause of the discontent, although the life of Huck Finn is not the only biography that partakes of the nature of fiction, and the Concord library would be further depleted if all biographies that are not true were cast out from it. . . .

Mr. Clemens has recently been elected a member of the Concord Free Trade club and in replying to the notice of election he takes care of himself in the following note:— Hartford, March 28, 1885. *Frank A. Nichols, Esq., Secretary Concord Free Trade Club:*— Dear Sir,—I am in receipt of your favor of the 24th instant, conveying the gratifying intelligence that I have been made an honorary member of the Free Trade Club of Concord, Massachusetts, and I desire to express to the club, through you, my grateful sense of the high compliment thus paid me. It does look as if Massachusetts were in a fair way to embarrass me with kindnesses this year. . . .

A committee of the public library of your town have condemned and excommunicated my last book and doubled its sale. This generous action of theirs must necessarily benefit me in one or two additional ways. For instance, it will deter other libraries from buying the book; and you are doubtless aware that one book in a public library prevents the sale of a sure ten and a possible hundred of its mates. And, secondly, it will cause the purchasers of the book to read it, out of curiosity, instead of merely intending to do so, after the usual way of the world and library committees; and then they will discover, to my great advantage and their own indignant disappointment, that there is nothing objectionable in the book after all.

And finally, the Free Trade Club of Concord comes forward and adds to the splendid burden of obligations already conferred upon me by the Commonwealth of Massachusetts, an honorary membership which is worth more than all the rest, just at this juncture, since it indorses me as worthy to associate with certain gentlemen whom even the moral icebergs of the Concord library committee are bound to respect. . . .

METHODS IN COMPOSITION

BY SAMUEL CLEMENS

In this reply to a question as to his methods in composition, Clemens very casually describes some very definite ideas about language and writing.

Your inquiry has set me thinking, but, so far, my thought fails to materialize. I mean that, upon consideration, I am not sure that I have methods in composition. I do suppose I have—I suppose I must have—but they somehow refuse to take shape in my mind; their details refuse to separate and submit to classification and description; they remain a jumble—visible, like the fragments of glass when you look in at the wrong end of a kaleidoscope, but still a jumble. If I could turn the whole thing around and look in at the other end, why then the figures would flash into form out of the chaos, and I shouldn't have any more trouble. But my head isn't right for that to-day, apparently. It might have been, maybe, if I had slept last night.

However, let us try guessing. Let us guess that whenever we read a sentence and like it, we unconsciously store it away in our model-chamber; and it goes with the myriad of its fellows to the building, brick by brick, of the eventual edifice which we call our style. And let us guess that whenever we run across other forms—bricks—whose colour, or some other defect, offends us, we unconsciously reject these, and so one never finds them in our edifice. If I have subjected myself to any training processes, and no doubt I have, it must have been in this unconscious or half-conscious fashion. I think it unlikely that deliberate and consciously methodical training is usual with the craft. I think it likely that the training most in use is of this unconscious sort, and is guided and governed and made by-and-by unconsciously systematic, by an automatically-working taste—a taste which selects and rejects without asking you for any help, and patiently and steadily improves itself without troubling you to approve or applaud. Yes, and likely enough when the structure is at last pretty well up, and attracts attention, *you* feel complimented, whereas you didn't build it, and didn't even consciously superintend. Yes; one notices, for instance, that long, involved sentences confuse him, and that he is obliged to re-read them to get the sense. Unconsciously, then, he rejects that brick. Unconsciously he accustoms himself to writing short sentences as a rule. At times he may indulge himself with a long one, but he will make sure that there are no folds in it, no vaguenesses, no parenthetical interruptions of its view as a whole; when he is done with it, it won't be a sea-serpent, with half of its arches under the water, it will be a torchlight procession.

Well, also he will notice in the course of time, as his reading goes on, that the difference between the *almost right* word and the *right* word is really a large matter—'tis the difference between the lightning-bug and the lightning. After that, of course, that exceedingly important brick, the *exact* word—however, this is running into an essay, and I beg pardon. So I seem to have arrived at this: doubtless I have methods, but they begot themselves, in which case I am only their proprietor, not their father.

TOM SAWYER, LIFE ON THE MISSISSIPPI, *and* HUCK FINN *established Mark Twain as a leading literary figure of his day. Although Clemens was able to recognize his enormous popularity, he never felt quite at ease with it. In his personal notebooks, he characterized his own books as water and those of the true geniuses of literature as wine. Still, he was quick to add, water is what everyone must drink. Above are four portraits featured in* McCLURE'S *magazine in the early 1880s. This period was the peak of Clemens's success as a writer and a publisher. In the years to come, he would find himself less able to concentrate on writing as he became more disturbed by the changes in the world around him and more deeply entangled in financial difficulties. Photo The Mark Twain House.*

FROM *A CONNECTICUT YANKEE IN KING ARTHUR'S COURT*

BY MARK TWAIN

The idea for A CONNECTICUT YANKEE *first entered Clemens's thoughts in Hawaii in the 1860s. He considered it again during one of his many trips to England and finally took it up in earnest in 1885. For the illustrations, he chose the work of artist Dan Beard. The first edition included 220 of Beard's illustrations. Illustration from* A CONNECTICUT YANKEE IN KING ARTHUR'S COURT, The Mark Twain House.

. . . *How he gets into King Arthur's realm, the author concerns himself as little as any of us do with the mechanism of our dreams. In fact the whole story has the lawless operation of a dream; none of its prodigies are accounted for: they take themselves for granted, and neither explain nor justify themselves. Here he is, that Connecticut man, foreman of one of the shops in Colt's pistol factory, and full to the throat of the invention and the self-satisfaction of the nineteenth century, at the court of the mythic Arthur. He is promptly recognized as a being of extraordinary powers, and becomes the king's right-hand man, with the title of The Boss; but as he has apparently no lineage or blazon, he has no social standing, and the meanest noble has precedence of him, just as would happen in England to-day. The reader may faintly fancy the consequences flowing from this situation, which he will find so vividly fancied for him in the book; but they are simply irreportable. The scheme confesses allegiance to nothing; the incidents, the facts follow as they will. The Boss cannot rest from introducing the apparatus of our time, and he tries to*

A CONNECTICUT YANKEE IN KING ARTHUR'S COURT appeared in 1889. The story centers around Hank Morgan, a Connecticut gentlemen who is knocked unconscious and wakes up in England in the days of King Arthur. Morgan uses his nineteenth-century knowledge to save himself from hanging and then goes on to rise to a position of great power. He modernizes the culture with innovations from his own day, but in the end nearly destroys it with modern weaponry. Part humorous storytelling and part angry diatribe, A CONNECTICUT YANKEE *is an allegorical attack on monarchy, class systems, organized religion, and slavery, and an indication of Clemens's growing uneasiness with the politics and culture of his own day. Here, Morgan awakens to find himself transported through time.*

The moment I got a chance I slipped aside privately and touched an ancient common looking man on the shoulder and said, in an insinuating, confidential way—

"Friend, do me a kindness. Do you belong to the asylum, or are you just here on a visit or something like that?"

He looked me over stupidly, and said—

"Marry, fair, sir, me seemeth—"

"That will do," I said; "I reckon you are a patient."

I moved away, cogitating, and at the same time keeping an eye out for any chance passenger in his right mind that might come along and give me some light. I judged I had found one, presently; so I drew him aside and said in his ear—

"If I could see the head keeper a minute—only just a minute—"

"Prithee do not let me."

"Let you *what?*"

"*Hinder* me, then, if the word please thee better." Then he went on to say he was an undercook and could not stop to gossip, though he would like it another time; for it would comfort his very liver to know where I got my clothes. As he started away he pointed and said yonder was one who was idle enough for my purpose, and was seeking me besides, no doubt. This was an airy slim boy in shrimp-colored tights that made him look like a forked carrot; the rest of his gear was blue silk and dainty laces and ruffles; and he had long yellow curls, and wore a plumed pink satin cap tilted complacently over his ear. By his look, he was good-natured; by his gait, he was satisfied with himself. He was pretty enough to frame. He arrived, looked me over with a smiling and impudent curiosity; said he had come for me and informed me that he was a page.

"Go 'long," I said; "You ain't more than a paragraph."

It was pretty severe, but I was nettled. However, it never phazed him; he didn't appear to know he was hurt. He began to talk and laugh, in happy, thoughtless, boyish fashion, as we walked along, and made himself old friends with me at once; asked me all sorts of questions about myself and about my clothes, but never waited for an answer—always chattered straight ahead, as if he didn't know he had asked a question and wasn't expecting any reply, until at last he happened to mention that he was born in the beginning of the year 513.

It made the cold chills creep over me! I stopped, and said, a little faintly:

"Maybe I didn't hear you just right. Say it again—and say it slow. What year was it?"

"Five thirteen."

"Five thirteen! You don't look it! Come, my boy, I am a stranger and friendless: be honest and honorable with me. Are you in your right mind?"

He said he was.

"Are these other people in their right minds?"

He said they were.

"And this isn't an asylum? I mean, it isn't a place where they cure crazy people?"

He said it wasn't.

"Well, then," I said, "either I am a lunatic, or something just as awful has happened. Now tell me, honest and true, where am I?"

"IN KING ARTHUR'S COURT."

I waited a minute, to let that idea shudder its way home, and then said:

"And according to your notions, what year is it now?"

"Five twenty-eight—nineteenth of June."

I felt a mournful sinking at the heart, and muttered: "I shall never see my friends again—never, never again. They will not be born for more than thirteen hundred years yet."

I seemed to believe the boy, I didn't know why. *Something* in me seemed to believe him—my consciousness, as you may say; but my reason didn't. My reason straightway began to clamor; that was natural. I didn't know how to go about satisfying it, because I knew that the testimony of men wouldn't serve—my reason would say they were lunatics and throw out their evidence. But all of a sudden I stumbled on the very thing, just by luck. I knew that the only total eclipse of the sun in the first half of the sixth century occurred on the twenty-first of June, A.D. 528 O.S., and began at three minutes after twelve noon. I also knew that no total eclipse of the sun was due in what to *me* was the present year—*i.e.*, 1879. So, if I could keep my anxiety and curiosity from eating the heart out of me for forty-eight hours, I should then find out for certain whether this boy was telling me the truth or not.

Wherefore, being a practical Connecticut man, I now shoved this whole problem clear out of my mind till its appointed day and hour should come, in order that I might turn all my attention to the circumstances of the present moment, and be alert and ready to make the most out of them that could be made. One thing at a time, is my motto—and just play that thing for all it is worth, even if it's only two pair and a jack. I made up my mind to two things; if it was still the nineteenth century and I was among lunatics and couldn't get away, I would presently boss that asylum or know the reason why; and if on the other hand it was really the sixth century, all right, I didn't want any softer thing: I would boss the whole country inside of three months; for I judged I would have the start of the best-educated man in the kingdom by a matter of thirteen hundred years and upwards. . . .

impart its spirit, with a thousand most astonishing effects. He starts a daily paper in Camelot; he torpedoes a holy well; he blows up a party of insolent knights with a dynamite bomb; when he and the king disguise themselves as peasants, in order to learn the real life of the people, and are taken and sold for slaves, and then sent to the gallows for the murder of their master, Lancelot arrives to their rescue with five hundred knights on bicycles. It all ends with the Boss's proclamation of the Republic after Arthur's death, and his destruction of the whole chivalry of England by electricity.

We can give no proper notion of the measureless play of an imagination which has a gigantic jollity in its feats, together with the tenderest sympathy. There are incidents in this wonder-book which wring the heart for what has been of cruelty and wrong in the past, and leave it burning with shame and hate for the conditions which are of like effect in the present. It is one of its magical properties that the fantastic fable of Arthur's far-off time is also too often the sad truth of ours; and the magician who makes us feel in it that we have just begun to know his power, teaches equality and fraternity in every phase of his phantasmagory.

He leaves, to be sure, little of the romance of the olden time, but no one is more alive to the simple, mostly tragic poetry of it; and we do not remember any book which imparts so clear a sense of what was truly heroic in it. With all his scorn of kingcraft, and all his ireful contempt of caste, no one yet has been fairer to the nobility of character which they cost so much too much to develop. The mainly ridiculous Arthur of Mr. Clemens has his moments of being as fine and high as the Arthur of Lord Tennyson; and the keener light which shows his knights and ladies in their childlike simplicity and their innocent coarseness throws all their best qualities into relief. This book is in its last effect the most matter-of-fact narrative, for it is always true to human nature, the only truth possible, the only truth essential, to fiction. The humor of the conception and of the performance is simply immense; but more than ever Mr. Clemens's humor seems the sunny break of his intense conviction. We must all recognize him here as first of those who laugh, not merely because his fun is unrivalled, but because there is a force of right feeling and clear thinking in it that never got into fun before.

from HARPER'S MAGAZINE, January 1890

Mark Twain

EUROPE AND THE WORLD
1890–1900

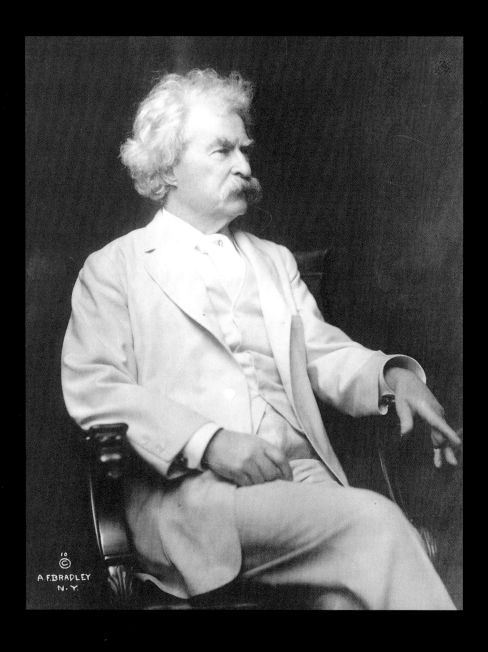

A.F.BRADLEY
N.Y.

The 1890s were a decade of trial and sadness for Samuel Clemens. He left behind his beloved house in Hartford, saw his wife's health begin to fail, struggled to pay great business debts, and lost his dear daughter Susy. Clemens spent much of the decade in Europe and on a world lecture tour as he fought to make money to pay his debts. He and his family chased after cures for a long string of ailments, including relief from their grief over Susy. Clemens returned to the United States in 1900 to begin anew in New York City; however, the trials of the previous decade had touched and forever altered the heart of Samuel Clemens and the voice of Mark Twain.

Illustration at right by Norman Rockwell from THE ADVENTURES OF TOM SAWYER, *1936 edition.*

GOODBYE TO HARTFORD

FROM *MR. CLEMENS AND MARK TWAIN*, BY JUSTIN KAPLAN

After two decades in Hartford, the Clemens family's lavish lifestyle finally proved incompatible with their rapidly failing finances, and they were forced to shut down their home. In the spring of 1891, the family sailed for France. Although they intended at the time to return, they would never again live in the house on Farmington Avenue. Biographer Justin Kaplan captures the sad mood that dominated as the Clemenses left behind their once-beloved home.

Stop street sprinkling—and electric lights—and publications—and clubs, three years—and pensions," Clemens reminded himself that spring [1891]; stop the telephone, sell the piano, the pew, the horses, find places for the butler and the coachman. Hamersley, the first of a long line of creditors he would eventually have to face, demanded his money back; the best Clemens could offer was a seventy-five-day note. He told Howells that for Livy's health they had decided to go to Europe for an indefinite stay, take the baths during the summer and spend winters in Berlin. It was a matter of necessity, he said. "Travel has no longer any charm for me. I have seen all the foreign countries I want to see except heaven and hell." Howells could have guessed another reason for going: the house had finally become too much for Clemens to keep up. After seventeen years the mansion on Farmington Avenue was stripped bare, furniture, carpets, and books had gone to the warehouse. Clemens' footsteps echoed in the empty rooms. Outside the conservatory door waited another symbol of Nook Farm's twilight: Harriet Beecher Stowe, holding flowers in her hands, smiled vaguely, and made strange noises. "This maniac," as he now called her, escaped daily from her hired Irish companion and wandered about frightening people with "her hideous gobblings."

"We are going to a world where there are no watermelons, and not much other food or cookery." On June 6, 1891, the Clemenses sailed for France on the *Gascoigne*, to be gone for more than eight of the next nine years and as a family never to live in Hartford again. On shipboard he wrote down some topics for the travel letters he had just contracted to write for the McClure Syndicate, and he added a familiar note of quite a different sort: "Tom and Huck die."

Memories of Susy, who died in 1896 from spinal meningitis, made life inside their Hartford home unthinkable for the Clemenses. In 1903, the house was sold to the president of the Hartford Fire Insurance Company. In the years to come it would be a boys' school, a warehouse, a public library, and a rooming house before the Mark Twain Memorial acquired the property in 1929 and began a historical restoration. Today, the home is maintained as a museum. At right, the Clemens family's home in the 1880s. Photo The Mark Twain House.

TROUBLE WITH BUSINESS

FROM *THE AUTOBIOGRAPHY OF MARK TWAIN*, EDITED BY CHARLES NEIDER

Clemens began his own publishing company in 1884 to avoid the many pitfalls of entrusting his work and his copyrights to others, and initially he had true success. This success was short-lived, however, and the company soon descended into a bitter bankruptcy from which Clemens would long struggle to recover. In this excerpt from his autobiography, Clemens describes the pain of the bankruptcy, as well as the salvation offered by Henry Huttleston Rogers, a man who would become one of his closest friends.

When the publishing house of Webster & Company failed, in the early '90's, its liabilities exceeded its assets by 66 per cent. I was morally bound for the debts, though not legally. The panic was on, business houses were falling to ruin everywhere, creditors were taking the assets—when there were any—and letting the rest go. Old business friends of mine said: "Business is business, sentiment is sentiment—and this is business. Turn the assets over to the creditors and compromise on that; other creditors are not getting 33 percent." Mr. Rogers was certainly a business man—no one doubts that. People who know him only by printed report will think they know what his attitude would be in the matter. And they will be mistaken. He sided with my wife. He was the only man who had a clear eye for the situation and could see that it differed from other apparently parallel situations. In substance he said this: "Business has its laws and customs and they are justified; but a literary man's reputation is his life; he can afford to be money poor but he cannot afford to be character poor; you must earn the cent per cent and pay it." My nephew, the late Samuel E. Moffet—himself a literary man—felt the same way, naturally enough; but I only mention him to recall and revivify a happy remark which he made and which traveled around the globe: "Honor knows no statute of limitations."

So it was decided. I must cease from idling and take up work again. I must write a book; also I must return to the lecture platform. My wife said I could clear off the load of debt in four years. Mr. Rogers was more cautious, more conservative, more liberal. He said that I could have as many years as I wanted—seven to start with. That was his joke. When he was not in the humor for pleasantry it was because he was asleep. Privately I was afraid his seven might be nearer the mark than Mrs. Clemens's four.

One day I got a shock—a shock which disturbed me a good deal. I overheard a brief conversation between Mr. Rogers and a couple of other seasoned men of affairs.

First Man of Affairs: "How old is Clemens?"

Mr. Rogers: "Fifty-eight."

First Man of Affairs: "Ninety-five percent of the men who fail at fifty-eight never get up again."

Second Man of Affairs: "You can make it ninety-eight per cent and be nearer right."

Those sayings haunted me for several days, troubling me with melancholy forbodings, and would not be reasoned away by me. There wasn't any room for reasoning, anyway, so far as I could see. If, at fifty-eight, ninety-eight men in a hundred who fail never get up again,

C. L. Webster and Co. published Mark Twain's greatest novel, ADVENTURES OF HUCKLEBERRY FINN, *and also produced one of the most widely read books of the era, the memoirs of former president of the United States and Civil War general Ulysses S. Grant. Grant was in failing health and in dire financial circumstances when he signed on with Webster and Co. and was to die before the memoirs were completed; but the book earned a generous sum of money for his widow and gave Webster and Co. a solid reputation among the country's leading publishers. Unfortunately for Clemens, this success was not to duplicate itself. Charles Webster, Clemens's business manager and the namesake of his publishing company, was the husband of Clemens's niece, Annie Moffet, and family ties more than personal affection brought the two men together. After the Grant memoirs, relations between Clemens and Webster fell apart, and the company sank deeper and deeper into debt. By the time Webster and Co. declared bankruptcy, Clemens and his nephew were no longer on speaking terms. Above, Charles Webster. Photo The Mark Twain House.*

what chance had I to draw No. 99 or No. 100? However, the depression did not last; it soon passed away, because Mrs. Clemens took her always-ready pencil and paper, when she learned my trouble, and clearly and convincingly ciphered out the intake of the four years and the resultant success. I could see that she was right. Indeed, she was always right. In foresight, wisdom, accurate calculation, good judgement and the ability to see all sides of a problem, she had no match among people I have known, except Mr. Rogers.

. . . [He] was in command, in the matter of creditors—and had been from the beginning. There were ninety-six creditors. He had meetings with them, discussions, arguments, persuasions, but no quarrels. Mrs. Clemens wanted to turn over to the creditors the house she had built in Hartford and which stood in her name, but he would not allow it. Neither would he allow my copyrights to go to them. Mrs. Clemens had lent the Webster firm $65,000 upon its notes in its perishing days, in the hope of saving its life, and Mr. Rogers insisted upon making her a preferred creditor and letting her have the copyrights in liquidation of the notes. He would not budge from this position and the creditors finally yielded the point.

Mr. Rogers insisted upon just two things besides the relinquishing of the copyrights: the creditors must be content with the Webster assets for the present and give me time to earn the rest of the firm's debt. He won them over. There was a clarity about his reasonings and a charm about his manner, his voice and the kindness and sincerity that looked out of his eyes that could win anybody that had brains in his head and a heart in his body. Of the ninety-six creditors only three or four stood out for rigorous and uncompromising measures against me and refused to relent. The others said I could go free and take my own time. They said they would obstruct me in no way and would bring no actions; and they kept their word. As to the three or four, I have never resented their animosity, except in my Autobiography. And even here not in spite, not in malice, but only frankly. It can never wound them, for I have every confidence that they will be in hell before it is printed.

The long, long head that Mr. Rogers carried on his shoulders! When he was so strenuous about my copyrights and so determined to keep them in the family I was not able to understand why he should think the matter so important. He insisted that they were a great asset. I said they were not an asset at all; I couldn't even *give* them away. He said, wait—let the panic subside and business revive and I would see; they would be worth more than they had ever been worth before. . . .

I am grateful to his memory for many a kindness and many a good service he did me but gratefulest of all for the saving of my copyrights—a service which saved me and my family from want and assured us permanent comfort and prosperity. . . .

Whereas he felt that Charlie Webster had failed him completely, Clemens made a new acquaintance in the 1890s who would restore his trust in his fellow man. Henry Huttleston Rogers was one of America's leading industrialists, a Standard Oil Company executive with personal wealth in the tens of millions. He was a self-made man with a reputation for ruthlessness in business. He was also an admirer of the works of Mark Twain. Clemens and Rogers met in 1893; not long afterward Rogers took control of Clemens's failing finances, steering him through bankruptcy proceedings, securing his copyrights for the future, and in the process becoming a dear and trusted friend. At left, a painting by J. Carroll Beckwith of Clemens in the 1890s. Photo The Mark Twain House.

MARK TWAIN, THE INVENTOR

FROM "MARK TWAIN AS INVENTOR," BY FRANCIS E. LEUPP, *HARPER'S WEEKLY*, 1901

Clemens was fascinated by technology and invention. In A CONNECTICUT YANKEE, *he considered what effect modern technology could have had in medieval England; and in a short story called "From the London* Times *of 1904" he created a device called the telelectroscope, which functioned much like the yet-to-be-invented television. In his real life as well, Clemens had an interest in invention, as this 1901 article describes.*

As the nineteenth century drew to an end, Clemens seemed to be aware that his life had become the subject of public fascination. Newspapers and magazines began detailing the "many sides" of Mark Twain, and the author himself began to focus a great deal on looking back. Above, Clemens poses for photographers as he looks out the window of his octagonal writing studio at Quarry Farm in Elmira, New York, in 1903. This was his final visit to the place where he had produced some of the most enduring works in American literature. The studio today sits on the campus of Elmira College as part of the school's Center for Mark Twain Studies. Photo The Mark Twain House.

A many-sided man indeed is Mark Twain. All the world knows him as author, for he has carried more than one generation of his countrymen to the verge of hysterics. . . . Half the world knows him as pioneer and editor, for his books are liberally peppered with his adventures in those capacities. A lesser class knows him as a pilot, for some of the best stories he ever wrote are connected with the old times on the Mississippi. The cabmen of New York know him as a civic reformer. A select group know him as a soldier, for he told them one night at dinner about his campaigns. How many know him as an inventor—not of facts, of course, but of things? Probably not a dozen employees of the Patent Office, for on their books he figures as plain Samuel L. Clemens, of Hartford. For all the note the clerks take of the hundreds of thousands of names which pass under their eyes, he might just as well have been John Smith, of Podunk Centre.

Yet here they are: A patent issued in December, 1871, for an "improvement in adjustable and detachable straps for garments," introduces us to the buckle-strap commonly used at the backs of waistcoats and trousers, but so made as to be buttoned on instead of sewed fast to the garment. Why any one who loves ease as well as Mark Twain should have wished to increase the labors of the toilet by needless unbuttoning and buttoning again is a mystery. He evidently does not care to solve it for us. With one of those whimsical twists which he cannot keep out of even the unpicturesque details of a business document, he leads the reader up to the point where inventors usually expatiate upon the special merits of their devices, and then says of his simply the advantages of such an adjustable strap "are so obvious that they need no explanation."

His second patent, granted two years later, we do find in use, though few persons who own a "Mark Twain scrap-book" suppose it to bear his name for any better reason than that which attaches the name of a noted man to a cigar or a travelling-bag. Come to think of it, though, is there not something mark-twainish about a scrap-book in which all the work of pasting is already done except furnishing the clippings?

There is a third patent, issued in 1885, for an invention far more elaborate than either of the others. This is described merely as a "game apparatus." . . .

Tradition in the Clemens family represents its most distinguished member as having, at one period in his life, cherished dreams of becoming a great inventor and amassing a fortune, just as Goethe aspired to science, Greeley to agriculture, and Nast to covering big canvases with historic battle-scenes. On the success of the *Jumping Frog* must rest the blame of checking the current of his career, and reducing him to his present unhappy state as the first of living humorists.

1894

Charles L. Webster & Co., MT's publishing company, declares bankruptcy.

1894

MT's PUDD'NHEAD WILSON *is published in November.*

1895

MT and his family return to New York City.

1895

The first American patent for a gasoline-powered vehicle is issued to Charles Duryea on June 11.

1895

THE RED BADGE OF COURAGE *by Stephen Crane is published.*

1895

MT begins a world lecture tour planned to earn the money to pay the debts of C. L. Webster & Co.

1896

The Supreme Court promotes the concept of "separate but equal" in racial segregation in its Plessy versus Ferguson *decision.*

1896

Prospectors strike gold near the Klondike River in Canada's Yukon Territory. The second great American gold rush begins the following spring when news of the Klondike gold reaches the United States.

1896

MT's JOAN OF ARC *is published.*

1896

MT lectures in Australia, India, and South Africa.

1896

Susy Clemens, MT's daughter, dies on August 18 in Hartford while the family is on a world lecture tour.

1897

MT and family live in London and Vienna.

Clemens poured hundreds of thousands of dollars into the inventions of others, most significantly a typesetter designed by James Paige. Clemens believed the machine would be the most significant innovation in printing since the invention of moveable type; but Paige's typesetter succeeded only in driving Clemens to the verge of financial ruin.

The Paige Compositor is known to Mark Twain's biographers as the most expensive of several ill-fated inventions in which Twain invested, including a steam pulley and a high-efficiency coal furnace.

Twain wasted at least $200,000 on the typesetting machine, which is often blamed for bringing him to the brink of bankruptcy in the mid 1890s. The Clemenses closed their Hartford home and headed for Europe in 1891, in part because of the financial strain of Twain's unprofitable investment.

Although the Paige episode is sometimes given as proof of Twain's poor judgement and lack of business acumen, engineers and newspaper compositors for a time were convinced—almost unanimously—that the machine was an engineering miracle destined to become standard equipment in the newspaper industry.

Four years ago a group of engineering and management students from Worcester Polytechnic Institute in Worcester, Mass., studied the only remaining Paige typesetter, which is on display at the Mark Twain Memorial. They also examined the mechanical drawings for the machine. Students and their advisers agreed: The Paige typesetter worked like a charm, but it just came too late to overtake the marketing success of the Mergenthaler Linotype machine which did become the industry standard.

"The machine worked, and worked efficiently," says Ken Ljunquist, a professor of American literature at the Worcester college, and one of the advisers of the Paige project. "The reasons for its failure were not mechanical. The Linotype just took over the market."

James W. Paige, a native of Rochester, N.Y., developed his idea for the machine in 1873 and took it to the Farnham Typesetting Manufacturing Co., located in the Colt Arms Factory in Hartford. . . . [In 1880] Twain met Paige, saw plans for his machine and bought $2,000 worth of stock in Farnham. A year later Paige developed a printing telegraph, which was successful, and Twain became Paige's biggest supporter. But slow progress on Paige's part discouraged the company, which dropped its backing for the typesetting machine in 1884.

Twain became Paige's primary backer in 1885, paying $2,000 a month to keep Paige at work. The machine was moved to the Hunt & Holbrook Building on Ann Street, and then to the Pratt & Whitney plant on Capitol Avenue. It was not finished until 1889, and Twain was in poor financial shape. By this time, Twain had turned down an offer from the Mergenthaler Linotype promoters to swap half their interests in the Linotype machine for a half interest in the Paige machine. The Mergenthaler offer indicated to Twain that his Paige machine was a sure winner.

Twain's dwindling resources led him to take his family to Europe in 1891, although he continued to hope the Paige machine would make him a millionaire.

The Paige machine, 9 feet long and weighing 3 tons, has 18,000 parts. Its 109-character keyboard was arranged so that entire words could be assembled by the operator in one stroke, using all fingers of both hands. At the end of each word, a word key was struck, and a line key was struck at the end of each line. While the operator continued to key in words, the words and lines already assembled in metal type were measured automatically and spaces of the proper thickness were automatically inserted to create perfectly justified columns. In addition, the machine would automatically reject broken type.

While a compositor could complete about 780 em spaces of justified type in an hour by hand (an em is the space occupied by the capital "M" in a given typeface), a Paige operator could produce nearly 12,000 ems an hour. Despite its weight, the machine was run by a 1/12th horsepower electric motor.

A group of newspaper executives and composing room foremen left Paige's 42 Union Place office on Jan. 29, 1892, convinced that they had seen a vision of the future after spending two days observing the machine.

The test observers, acting as a committee of the American Newspaper Publishers Association, called the Paige Compositor "the mechanical marvel of the 19th century."

"From the reports available, regarding other machines in the field, I have little doubt of the success of the Paige Compositor," wrote W. G. Cox, foreman of the composing room at the New Haven *Register*, who was at the Hartford test. "The Paige Compositor has captured me entirely," wrote W. H. Helmle, composing room foreman at the Brooklyn (N.Y.) *Times*.

In a test of the Paige machine at the Chicago *Herald* (which was the only company to make commercial use of the machine), it outperformed 32 linotype machines.

But Linotype's promoters outperformed Paige and Twain. Only two of the complicated Paige machines were produced. Paige kept technical details to himself and never fully trained technicians for the machine. By tinkering with his machine, he lost critical time to Linotype. There were 55 Linotype machines in operation in 1887, just two years before the Paige machine was completed. But by 1895, there were 1,076 Linotypes in operation—they had become standard newspaper publishing equipment.

At the advice of Henry H. Rogers, who had taken over management of Twain's troubled finances, Twain bailed out of the Paige machine in 1894.

In a letter to Twain, Rogers said the machine was everything Twain said it was—but that it was still a bad investment. Twain needed every penny to repay the creditors of his bankrupt publishing firm, Charles L. Webster & Co. of New York. Twain spent four years lecturing throughout the world and finished paying his debts in 1898. . . .

Only two working models of the Paige Compositor were ever produced: one in 1887 and another in 1894. The 1887 model is now in the Mark Twain House in Hartford. The other was given to Cornell University. During World War II, with the demand great for scrap metal, Cornell donated the machine to the government, and it was melted down for the war effort. Below, the Paige Compositor at The Mark Twain House. Photo The Mark Twain House.

AROUND THE WORLD

SAMUEL CLEMENS, FROM THE WORLD LECTURE TOUR, 1895

Clemens's book about his world lecture tour, FOLLOW-
ING THE EQUATOR, was the last of his five travel books;
and unlike those that came before, it was mostly fac-
tual, with little of the exaggeration, embellishment,
and embroidery that had become Mark Twain's
trademark. FOLLOWING THE EQUATOR is, overall, a
more serious book than the earlier travel volumes,
with discussions of labor issues, economic policies,
and history. The comparatively somber tone of the
book is likely the result of both the serious financial
troubles that made the lecture tour necessary and of
the terrible loss that cast a shadow over its composi-
tion. In August of 1896, only weeks after Clemens
gave his final lecture, he learned that his daughter
Susy had died in Hartford. Clemens struggled
through his grief to complete the book, but he never
fully recovered from the staggering blow of losing his
beloved daughter at such a young age. Below,
Clemens in 1895, at the outset of his world lecture
tour. Photo The Mark Twain House.

The bankruptcy that destroyed his publishing company in 1894 left Clemens deeply in debt.
Determined to pay every penny that the company owed, Clemens agreed to a 140-date world
lecture tour under the management of J. B. Pond. Accompanied by Livy and Clara, Clemens
began the tour in Cleveland in 1895 and then made his way toward the West Coast. From
there he sailed to Australia, then on to New Zealand, India, and South Africa, completing
the tour in July of 1896. The tour, and the book that Clemens wrote about it, FOLLOWING
THE EQUATOR, earned enough money to satisfy his creditors and also marked the end of his
professional lecturing career.

I was solicited to go around the world on a lecture tour by a man in Australia. I asked him what they wanted to be lectured on. He wrote back that those people were very coarse, and serious, and that they would like something solid, something gigantic; and he proposed that I prepare about three or four lectures at any rate, on just morals, any kind of morals, but just moral, and I liked that idea. I liked it very much and was perfectly willing to engage in that kind of work, and I should like to teach morals. I have great enthusiasm in doing that, and I shall like to teach morals to those people. I do not like to have them taught to me, and I do not know of any duller entertainment than that, but I know I can produce a quality of goods that will satisfy those people.

If you teach principles, why, you had better let your illustrations come first, illustrations which shall carry home to every person. I planned my first lecture on morals. I must not stand here and talk all night; get out a watch: I am talking the first time now, and I do not know anything about the length of it. . . .

I thought I would state a principle which I was going to teach. I have this theory for doing a great deal of good out there, everywhere in fact, that you should prize as a priceless thing every transgression, every crime that you commit—the lesson of it, I mean.

Make it permanent; impress it so that you may never commit that same crime again as long as you live; then you will see yourself what the logical result of that will be—that you get interested in committing crimes. You will lay up in that way, course by course, the edifice of a personally perfect moral character. You cannot afford to waste any crime; they are not given to you to be thrown away, but for a great purpose. There are 462 crimes possible, and you cannot add anything to this; you cannot originate anything. These have been all thought out, all experimented on, and have been thought out by the most capable men in the penitentiary. When you commit a transgression, lay it up in your memory, . . . and it will all lead to moral perfection. When you have committed your 462 you are released of every possibility and have ascended the staircase of faultless creation, and you finally stand with your 462 complete with absolute moral perfection, and I am more than two-thirds up there. It is immense inspiration to find yourself climbing that way, with not much further to go. . . . Why, the first time I ever stole a watermelon—I think it was the first time, but this is no matter, it was right along there somewhere—I carried that watermelon to a secluded bower. You may call it a bower, and I suppose you may not. I carried that watermelon to a secluded bower in the lumber yard, and broke it open, and it was green.

Now then, I began to reflect—that is the beginning of reformation, when you reflect. When you do not reflect, that transgression is wasted on you. I began to reflect, and I said to myself: Now, what would a right-minded and right-intentioned boy do, who found that he had done wrong—stolen a watermelon like this. What would he do—what must he do? Do right; restitution; make restitution. He must restore that property to its owner; and I resolved to do that, and the moment I made that good resolution I felt that electrical moral uplift which becomes a victory over wrongdoing. I was spiritually strengthened and refreshed, and carried that watermelon back to that wagon and gave it to the farmer—restored it to him—and I told him he ought to be ashamed of himself going around working off green watermelons in that way on people who had confidence in him, and I told him in my perfectly frank manner it was wrong. I told him if he did not stop he could not have my custom and he was ashamed. He was ashamed; he said he would never do it again, and I believe that I did that man a good turn, as well as one for myself. He did reform; I was severe with him a little, but that was all. I restored the watermelon and made him give me a ripe one. I morally helped him, and I have no doubt that I helped myself the same time, for that was a lesson which remained with me for my perfection. Ever since that day to this I never stole another one—like that.

When his world lecture tour was completed and his debts were paid, Clemens vowed he would never lecture again. James Pond, the man who had managed his world tour as well as the earlier tour with George Washington Cable, tried to lure Clemens out of retirement with an offer of fifty thousand dollars for a tour of the United States, but Clemens remained firm. In the years to come, he would occasionally give a public speech, but never again would he return to the lecture circuit. After the world tour, the Clemenses lived in England and in Vienna before returning permanently to the United States. At left, Clemens in 1898. Photo The Mark Twain House.

After an absence of five years Mr. S. L. Clemens (Mark Twain) returns to his home from "a tour around the world to pay his debts." . . .

On the 15th of July, 1895, he began his tour in Cleveland. The great Music Hall there gave him a send-off with an audience of over 3,000 people who packed the building, on a mid-July night, with the mercury in the nineties. He had been very ill, subject to many annoyances from being dragged from a sick bed to appear in supplementary proceedings in New York the day before starting, and suffering from a huge carbuncle that had kept him confined to his home for seven weeks.

In my announcement of the tour across the continent "Mark" suggested to me that traveling around the world was nothing, as everybody did that, but what he was traveling for was unusual; everybody didn't do that.

From Cleveland he went by the steamers NORTHLAND and NORTHWEST to Duluth, Minn., and St. Paul and Winnipeg, and over the Great Northern route to Puget Sound, Vancouver, and Victoria, B.C., where he sailed on the 21st day of August by steamship Warrimoo for Australia, having delivered twenty-four lectures in twenty-two cities.

It was not until we reached Great Falls, Mon., half way across the continent, that Mark was able to leave his hotel, except as he was driven to and from the lecture hall or took a short walk, but a greater exhibition of courage and determination I never witnessed than in these struggles from day to day to carry through the work he had planned for ridding himself of the bondage of debt. . . .

I consider Mark Twain one of the greatest geniuses of our time. I think I know him better than he is known to most men—wide as his circle of acquaintance is, big as his reputation is. He is as great a man as he is a genius, too. Tenderness and sensitiveness are his two strongest traits. He has one of the best hearts that ever beat. One must know him well to fully discern all of his best traits. I sometimes think that he fights shy of having it generally suspected that he is kind and tender-hearted, but many of his friends do know it. . . .

J. B. Pond, from THE NEW YORK TIMES, October 20, 1900

The Early Twilight

from Mr. Clemens and Mark Twain, by Justin Kaplan

1897

FOLLOWING THE EQUATOR, *the account of MT's world lecture tour, is published in November.*

1897

Orion Clemens, MT's older brother, dies in December.

1898

The United States battleship MAINE *explodes in Havana harbor in February, killing 260 men. The ship was there to protect American investments in Cuba during the island's rebellion against Spanish occupation.*

1898

The tension between the United States and Spain over Cuban independence erupts into war.

1898

The annexation of Hawaii is approved by the United States Congress.

1898

The Spanish-American War comes to an end, leaving the United States in possession of Puerto Rico and Guam and paving the way for American occupation of the Philippines.

1898

H. H. Rogers informs MT that his creditors are paid in full.

1899

Jean Clemens, MT's youngest child, receives treatment for epilepsy in Sweden.

1899

Philippine guerrillas revolt against American occupation forces.

1899

MT's story "The Man That Corrupted Hadleyburg" is published in December.

1900

MT returns to America in October, settling in New York City.

The last years of the nineteenth century were full of sadness and despair for Samuel Clemens. The bankruptcy of his publishing company, the sudden death of his daughter, and the failing health of his wife cast a dark shadow over his days. Justin Kaplan compares Clemens's condition with that of his country as the new century approached.

For both Mark Twain and his America the frontier was closed. That "great historic movement" which Frederick Jackson Turner, reading his celebrated paper to his fellow historians in 1893, said had come to an end in America had also come to an end in Mark Twain. Like his country, which he eventually symbolized for many, he was at an age when he could no longer afford to be prodigal. In 1861, roughing it on the shores of Lake Tahoe, he had carelessly started a forest fire. He had been intoxicated by the spectacle, described it as "superb! magnificent! beautiful!" "Blazing banners" of flame, a hundred feet in the air, roared through the forest, were reflected in the lake, climbed up and over the mountain and left a charred wasteland behind. As a writer he judged his craft by the same standard of gaudy, profligate spectacle: he liked effects that worked like Fourth of July rockets or a torchlight procession. His writing table and manuscript trunk could never hold the projects he began in a forest fire of enthusiasm and then put aside, when the flames stopped leaping, in favor of some other conflagration. Like America's untouched forests and inexhaustible herds of buffalo, there was always more where the first or fiftieth or hundredth came from.

Now, in the early twilight of his life, having suffered frightful affronts to his sense of plenitude and possibility, he felt frugality and defensiveness forced upon him, conservation, limits, self-inquiry, inwardness. He was no longer working a bonanza claim. He had already struck barren rock, had seen the failure of his frontier talent for improvising a way out of trouble and of his frontier faith that things will always come out right in the long run. In 1897 an American paper ran a headline five columns wide, "Close of a Great Career," and under it the baseless story that Mark Twain, abandoned by his wife and daughters, was living in abject poverty. He raged in disgust after he read it. Only a man, he said, could be capable of such lying and vileness, not a dog or a cow. But he knew that his luck, which he trusted all his life, had finally run out, even though he was far from poverty, and one day that winter he wrote out a list to prove it: the cook's sweetheart was dying, one of the maids might go blind, the porter had pleurisy, a friend's baby had died, another friend had fractured his skull, and on the way back from a visit to him in the hospital Clemens' cab had nearly run over a little boy. "Since bad luck struck us," he concluded from all this, "it is risky for people to have to do with us."

In order to reach a kind of accommodation with the guilt and casualty that seemed to be his daily bread, he began to write what he thought of as his "Bible," a one-sided Socratic dialogue called *What Is Man?* He believed that it was theological dynamite, that all the creeds which gave dignity to man and God would crumble under the force of its angry logic. Livy loathed it, shuddered over it, would not even listen to the last half, much less permit him to publish any part of it. He published the book only after her death, and even then privately and, he believed, anonymously. But its despairing ideas dominated his conversation from 1897 on. His children and friends dreaded the inevitable monologue of gloom and vituperation, and one of Livy's consolations, maybe even one of her motives, as she spent more and more time isolated in a sickroom, was that she was spared these performances.

FROM "THE MAN THAT CORRUPTED HADLEYBURG"
BY MARK TWAIN

"The Man That Corrupted Hadleyburg" showcases a darker side of Mark Twain, albeit one not minus the humor. The story concerns a man who, having been slighted on a trip through the town of Hadleyburg—a town that trumpets its reputation as "the most honest and upright town"—devises a scheme to repay the town for their disregard by turning their own pious self-righteousness against them. Clemens wrote the story while living in Vienna, after his world lecture tour and before his return to the United States.

I t was many years ago. Hadleyburg was the most honest and upright town in all the region round about. It had kept that reputation unsmirched during three generations, and was prouder of it than of any other of its possessions. It was so proud of it, and so anxious to insure its perpetuation, that it began to teach the principles of honest dealing to its babies in the cradle, and made the like teachings the staple of their culture thenceforward through all the years devoted to their education. Also, throughout the formative years temptations were kept out of the way of the young people, so that their honesty could have every chance to harden and solidify, and become a part of their very bone. The neighboring towns were jealous of this honorable supremacy, and affected to sneer at Hadleyburg's pride in it and call it vanity; but all the same they were obliged to acknowledge that Hadleyburg was in reality an incorruptible town; and if pressed they would also acknowledge that the mere fact that a young man hailed from Hadleyburg was all the recommendation he needed when he went forth from his natal town to seek for responsible employment.

But at last, in the drift of time, Hadleyburg had the ill luck to offend a passing stranger— possibly without knowing it, certainly without caring, for Hadleyburg was sufficient unto itself, and cared not a rap for strangers or their opinions. Still, it would have been well to make an exception in this one's case, for he was a bitter man and revengeful. All through his wanderings during a whole year he kept his injury in mind, and gave all his leisure moments to trying to invent a compensating satisfaction for it. He contrived many plans, and all of them were good, but none of them was quite sweeping enough; the poorest of them would hurt a great many individuals, but what he wanted was a plan which would comprehend the entire town, and not let so much as one person escape unhurt. At last he had a fortunate idea, and when it fell into his brain it lit up his whole head with an evil joy. He began to form a plan at once, saying to himself, "That is the thing to do—I will corrupt the town."

Travel became a way of life for Clemens after he and his family left Hartford in 1891. Financial troubles and family tragedy seemed to shadow his every step, however, and peace proved elusive. Below, Clemens sits outside the cottage in Lee, Massachusetts, where he spent the months immediately following the death of his wife in the summer of 1904. The pastoral beauty of the place offered little solace. During Clemens's brief stay in Lee, his daughter Jean was seriously hurt in a riding accident; soon thereafter, Clemens left Lee for New York City. Photo The Mark Twain House.

Mark Twain

THE FINAL YEARS
1900–1910

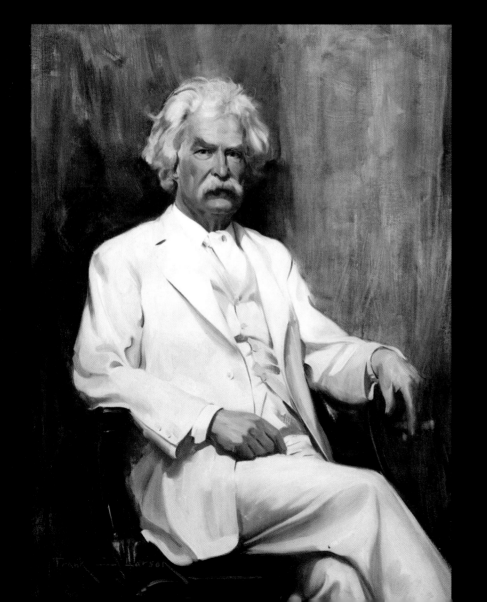

In his final decade, Samuel Clemens lived in New York City and at a home called Stormfield in southern Connecticut. As his life drew to a close, he led the strange existence of a living icon: his opinion was sought on all matters and his image—brilliant white suits and wild white hair—became unmistakable and inescapable. The author spent much of his time looking backward—in speeches and essays recounting his life and in long-winded sessions with his biographer—and his last days were touched by great sadness as he said goodbye to both his wife Livy and his youngest daughter Jean. But Clemens also knew great fulfillment as he saw his life and works embraced wholeheartedly by the American people. When Clemens died on April 21, 1910, the country had grown beyond recognition since the year of his birth. The American Union now numbered forty-six states and stretched from the Atlantic to the Pacific. And in the night skies, Halley's Comet was back again for the first time since Clemens's birth; observers noted that it shone far more brilliantly to mark the author's passing than it had to greet his arrival.

Illustration at right by Norman Rockwell from ADVENTURES OF
HUCKLEBERRY FINN, *1940 edition*

THE MOST CONSPICUOUS PERSON ON THE PLANET

FROM *MARK TWAIN AND HIS WORLD*, BY JUSTIN KAPLAN

1900

The population of the United States is recorded at 75,994,575.

1900

SISTER CARRIE by Theodore Dreiser is published.

1900

MT arrives in New York City after nearly a decade of foreign residence.

1901

The Philippine rebellion against American occupation is ended. Later in the year the islands are declared "unorganized territory" of the United States.

1901

President Theodore Roosevelt defines his foreign policy with the phrase "speak softly and carry a big stick."

1901

MT's essay "To the Person Sitting in Darkness" is published.

1901

MT receives an honorary degree from Yale University.

1901

MT moves from New York City to the town of Riverdale.

1901

MT meets his future biographer, Albert Bigelow Paine.

1902

The Hartford house, home to MT and his family for nearly twenty years, is put on the market.

1902

Olivia Clemens becomes seriously ill.

1903

MT takes his family to Italy; they return to the U.S. the following year.

1904

Olivia Langdon Clemens, wife of MT, dies in Florence, Italy, in June.

When Clemens returned to America after nearly a decade abroad, he was met with a warm welcome. Not only was he one of the nation's favorite authors, he was also a man of "commercial honor" as THE NEW YORK TIMES *called him, celebrated for his personal efforts to pay off the business debts that had thrown his publishing company into bankruptcy. For this act, Clemens was held up as an example of the finest American character.*

I come back from my exile young again, fresh and alive, and ready to begin life once more," Clemens said in November 1900 at a New York dinner in his honor. Vigorous, playful, and smiling as he stepped off the gangplank of the steamship *Minnehaha* . . . he had come home to an ovation that was to go on for the rest of his life. Newspapers all over the country hailed the return of "the bravest author in all literature" and followed the lead of the *New York Times* in paying tribute to "the Hero as Man of Letters" and to a national morality solidly based on commercial honor. "It is a great thing to possess genius," the Boston *Weekly Transcript* said; "it is a greater thing to be a man of unsullied honor." Mark Twain was as funny as ever, one reporter noted, but a little better-natured than he used to be. Now, instead of dodging interviewers, he freely discussed with the press his belief that "the trouble with us in America is that we haven't learned to speak the truth," and he outlined his short-range plans to spend the winter in New York (which he conceded was "cleaner than Bombay"), to work and travel as little as possible, and to run for President on the broad platform of being in favor of everything.

Settled in at a furnished house on West Tenth Street, he received a stream of visitors who solicited his opinions on heaven and hell, the Boer War and the Boxer Rebellion, and his favorite method of escaping from the Indians. "It always puzzled me," his daughter Clara recalled, "how Mark Twain could manage to have an opinion on every incident, accident, invention, or disease in the world." He set out on a round of lunches, club banquets, speeches, and public appearances that at first nearly devoured him and left him exhausted after the almost nightly "dreadful ordeal" of dinner music, clashing cutlery, and shrieking human voices rising in competition with one another toward sheer pandemonium. Howells commented, "I hate to see him eating so many dinners and writing so few books." Yet the sufficient reward of these occasions for Mark Twain was love, homage, and the moment when he rose to speak and give play to his spellbinding presence and personality.

"The most satisfying and spirit-exalting honor done me in all my seventy years, oh, by seventy times seventy!" he was to say of the birthday celebration at Delmonico's on 5 December 1905. There, against a background of potted palms, gilt mirrors, and the music of a forty-piece orchestra from the Metropolitan Opera House, Colonel George Harvey, president of Harper and Brothers, had assembled what was in effect a living tableau of Mark Twain's years in the East: writers like Howells and Cable; old friends like Twichell; the plutocrats Rogers and Andrew Carnegie; editors, critics, humorists; respectable, workaday literary practitioners who would soon be forgotten but were now the night sky for the brilliance of Mark Twain's departing comet. In his funny and sad speech, neither the first nor the last of his series of swan songs, he looked back over the seventy years since his birth in "a little hamlet, in the backwoods of Missouri, where nothing ever happened," and he joked about his morals ("an acquirement—like music, like a foreign language, like piety, poker, paralysis") and his habits. "It has always been my rule never to smoke when asleep, and never to refrain when awake," he said, but confessed, "I have stopped smoking now and then, for a few months at a time, but it was not on principle, it was only to show off; it was to pulverize those critics who said I was a slave to my habits and couldn't break my bonds." The lesson of all this was, "We can't reach old age by another man's road. My habits protect my life, but they would assassinate you." Having reached "Pier Number Seventy," he was prepared, he told his hearers—and he believed it himself for the moment—to sail again "toward the sinking sun" with "a reconciled spirit" and "a contented heart."

On the streets and in theatres and restaurants Mark Twain was so often pointed out and applauded that, as Clara said, "it was difficult to realize he was only a man of letters." He had, in fact, become something more—sage, oversoul, spokesman, and a hero of a distinctly antiheroic and vernacular sort. His career had followed a mythic pattern of journey from obscurity and poverty in Hannibal, mortal struggle, victory, and return. His fame had also been affected by a series of revolutions in the printing and distribution of news and in the public appetite for news. He became, without parallel or equal, a celebrity—in Daniel Boorstin's definition, "a person who is known for his well-knownness." He was to be the subject of countless news stories which, by the dynamics of celebrity and through his own brilliant management, made him even better copy and brought him closer to realizing his declared ambition to be the "most conspicuous person on the planet." And he may actually have realized this ambition in June 1907, when he journeyed to England (he would have been even willing "to journey to Mars," he said) to receive the degree of Doctor of Literature from Oxford and the robe of scarlet and gray which he cherished and flaunted from then on.

The reporters who dogged his steps wherever he went were attracted not so much by his literature as by his vividness and his genius for generating news and "effects" (like his Connecticut Yankee), his astonishing opinions and mannerisms, his mane of white hair which he washed with soap each morning, and the white suits that he took to wearing after 1906. That December, standing up to testify before a joint committee on copyright in Washington, he stripped off his long overcoat. Dressed from shoulder to foot in white serge, he was like a blaze of sunlight in the dimly lighted room at the Library of Congress. Then, as he had been doing for years, he spoke out, like Charles Dickens, in defense of intellectual property rights and in anticipation of the happy day when, as he had said long before, "in the eyes of the law, literary property will be as sacred as whiskey, or any other of the necessaries of life."

His dazzling white outfits made him, he claimed, "absolutely the only cleanly clothed human being in all Christendom north of the Tropics." But in their assertion of an inner purity as well (Howells called him "whited sepulchre") the famous white suits answered to a lifetime hunger for love and expiation. White was the garb of publicness for Mark Twain, just as it had been the garb of reclusiveness for Emily Dickinson. Dressed in white he would walk up Fifth Avenue to Fifty-ninth Street on a Sunday morning and rest in the lobby of the Plaza Hotel until the churches were out; then he walked homeward along sidewalks crowded with fashionable strangers who lifted their hats to him in recognition and homage. "It was his final harvest," said his biographer, who accompanied him on these walks, "and he had the courage to claim it."

The white suit that we so readily attribute to Mark Twain was not a part of Clemens's wardrobe until he was seventy-one years old, and even then he wore it only occasionally—and only once while speaking in public. Obsessed with cleanliness and always ready to create a stir, Clemens certainly loved the incongruity of a sparkling white suit on a winter day in New York City; but it was the Mark Twain impersonators who flourished after his death, most influentially Hal Holbrook, who made the white suit part of the definitive uniform of Mark Twain. Above, a VANITY FAIR cartoon depicts the classic Mark Twain. Photo The Mark Twain House. Below, Clemens in 1904. Photo The Mark Twain Memorial.

THE SEVENTIETH BIRTHDAY

FROM MARK TWAIN'S SEVENTIETH BIRTHDAY SPEECH, DECEMBER 5, 1905

New York City was an appropriate place to celebrate the completion of Clemens's seventh decade of life. When the author and his family returned from nearly a decade abroad in 1900, it was in New York that they made their home; and four years later, when Clemens lost his wife, Olivia, he took up residence in an apartment on Fifth Avenue. It was there, in the heart of Manhattan, that Clemens became what biographer Justin Kaplan justly called "the most conspicuous person on the planet." Two years before his death, Clemens left New York for Redding, Connecticut, but remained drawn to the life of the city. He made his final visit only a week before his death. Above, Clemens at seventy. Photo The Mark Twain House.

1904
MT's sister, Pamela Clemens Moffett, dies in August.

1905
MT dines with President Theodore Roosevelt at the White House.

1905
MT rents a house for the summer in Dublin, New Hampshire.

A celebration in honor of Samuel Clemens's seventieth birthday drew a pack of celebrities, including Andrew Carnegie, Willa Cather, and William Dean Howells, and featured a lively speech, excerpted below, by the guest of honor.

The seventieth birthday! It is the time of life when you arrive at a new and awful dignity; when you may throw aside the decent reserves which have oppressed you for a generation and stand unafraid and unabashed upon your seven-terraced summit and look down and teach—unrebuked. You can tell the world how you got there. It is what they all do. You shall never get tired of telling by what delicate arts and deep moralities you climbed up to that great place. You will explain the process and dwell on the particulars with senile rapture. I have been anxious to explain my own system this long time, and now at last I have the right.

I have achieved my seventy years in the usual way: by sticking strictly to a scheme of life which would kill anybody else. It sounds like an exaggeration, but that is really the common rule for attaining to old age. When we examine the program of any of these garrulous old people we always find that the habits which have preserved them would have decayed us; that the way of life which enabled them to live upon the property of their heirs so long, as Mr. Choate says, would have put us out of commission ahead of time. I will offer here, as a sound maxim, this: That we can't reach old age by another man's road.

I will now teach, offering my way of life to whomsoever desires to commit suicide by the scheme which has enabled me to beat the doctor and the hangman for seventy years. Some of the details may sound untrue, but they are not. I am not here to deceive; I am here to teach.

We have no permanent habits until we are forty. Then they begin to harden, presently they petrify, then business begins. Since forty I have been regular about going to bed and getting up—and that is one of the main things. I have made it a rule to go to bed when there wasn't anybody left to sit up with; and I have made it a rule to get up when I had to. This has resulted in an unswerving regularity of irregularity. It has saved me sound, but it would injure another person.

In the matter of diet—which is another main thing—I have been persistently strict in sticking to the things which didn't agree with me until one or the other of us got the best of it. Until lately I got the best of it myself. But last spring I stopped frolicking with mince pie after midnight; up to then I had always believed it wasn't loaded. For thirty years I have taken coffee and bread at eight in the morning, and no bite nor sup until seven-thirty in the evening. Eleven hours. That is all right for me, and is wholesome, because I have never had a headache in my life, but headachy people would not reach seventy comfortably by that road, and they would be foolish to try it. And I wish to urge upon you this—which I think is wisdom—that if you find you can't make seventy by any but an uncomfortable road, don't you go. When they take off the Pullman and retire you to the rancid smoker, put on your things, count your checks, and get out at the first way station where there's a cemetery. . .

I desire now to repeat and emphasize that maxim: We can't reach old age by another man's road. My habits protect my life but they would assassinate you. . . .

THE PRODUCT OF A MAN'S LABOR

FROM A SPEECH TO CONGRESS, DECEMBER 8, 1905, BY MARK TWAIN

Throughout his career, Clemens fought to preserve his own copyrights; and at the end of his life-time, he worked to secure better copyright laws for all writers. Three times he appeared before Congress to testify on the subject. In December of 1905, he used the commandment "Thou shalt not steal" to illustrate his point about the pirating of authors' works.

I have read this bill. At least I have read such portions as I could understand. Nobody but a practiced legislator can read the bill and thoroughly understand it, and I am not a practiced legislator. I am interested particularly and especially in the part of the bill which concerns my trade. I like that extension of copyright life to the author's life and fifty years afterward. I think that would satisfy any reasonable author, because it would take care of his children. Let the grandchildren take care of themselves. That would take care of my daughters, and after that I am not particular. I shall then have long been out of this struggle. . . . I am aware that copyright must have a limit, because that is required by the Constitution of the United States, which sets aside the earlier constitution, which we call the decalogue. The decalogue says you shall not take away from any man his profit. I don't like to use harsh terms. What the decalogue really says is "Thou shalt not steal," but I am trying to use more polite language.

The laws of England and America do take it away, do select but one class, the people who create the literature of the land. They always talk handsomely about the literature of the land, always what a fine, great, monumental thing a great literature is, and in the midst of their enthusiasm, they turn around and do what they can to discourage it.

I know we must have a limit, but forty-two years is too much of a limit. I am quite unable to guess why there should be a limit at all to the possession of the product of a man's labor. There is no limit to real estate. Dr. Hale has suggested that a man might just as well, after discovering a coal mine and working it forty-two years, have the government step in and take it away.

What is the excuse? Is it that the author who produced that book has had the profit of it long enough, and therefore the government takes a profit which does not belong to it and generously gives it to the 88,000,000 of people. But it doesn't do anything of the kind. It merely takes the author's property, takes his children's bread and gives the publisher double profit. He goes on publishing the book and as many of his confederates as choose to go into the conspiracy do so, and they rear families in affluence. And they continue the enjoyment of those ill-gotten gains generation after generation forever, for they never die. In a few weeks or months or years I shall be out if it, I hope under a monument. I hope I shall not be entirely forgotten, and shall subscribe to the monument myself. But I shall not be caring what happens if there are fifty years left of my copyright. My copyright produces annually a good deal more than I can use, but my children can use it. I can get along; I know a lot of trades. But that goes to my daughters, who can't get along as well as I can because I have carefully raised them as young ladies, who don't know anything and can't do anything. I hope Congress will extend to them the charity they have failed to get from me.

In 1908, Clemens established the Mark Twain Company and assigned to it all his copyrights and the use of his pen name. An outgrowth of the Mark Twain Company is the Mark Twain Project at the University of California at Berkeley, which today controls many of Mark Twain's copyrights and is publishing his letters in a multiple volume edition. Above, Thomas Nast depicts Clemens caught up in the struggle over international copyright law; The Mark Twain House.

SPEAKING FROM THE GRAVE

FROM *MR. CLEMENS AND MARK TWAIN*, BY JUSTIN KAPLAN

AN ALTERNATE
...for those who prefer a work of non-fiction
instead of—or in addition to—the current Selection

THE AUTOBIOGRAPHY OF
MARK TWAIN

AN AMERICAN CLASSIC IN READABLE FORM FOR
THE FIRST TIME – INCLUDING MORE THAN
30,000 WORDS OF TEXT NEVER BEFORE IN PRINT
AND PHOTOGRAPHS NEVER BEFORE PUBLISHED

Edited by Charles Neider

(REGULAR RETAIL PRICE: $6.00) PRICE TO MEMBERS: $4.95

BOOK-DIVIDEND CREDIT GIVEN WITH THIS PURCHASE

Albert Paine was not only Clemens's biographer, but, in the last months of the author's life, his closest companion. Paine's biography appeared in 1912 as a three-volume work entitled MARK TWAIN, A BIOGRAPHY. *His version of Clemens's autobiography,* MARK TWAIN'S AUTOBIOGRAPHY, *appeared in 1924. For many years, Paine was the only scholar to have access to the wealth of Clemens's autobiographical material; but after Paine's death, Bernard Devoto took over as editor of the foundation that controlled Clemens's writings and put together his own volume of Clemens's autobiographical writings,* MARK TWAIN IN ERUPTION *(1940). Almost twenty years later, Charles Neider assembled what he called* THE AUTOBIOGRAPHY OF MARK TWAIN, *a collection of Clemens's dictated material organized into chronological order to approximate a true autobiography. Another volume of biography drawn from Clemens's dictated material appeared in the early 1990s, and yet another is slated for publication in 1998. Above, the cover of Charles Neider's version of* THE AUTOBIOGRAPHY OF MARK TWAIN. *Photo The Mark Twain House.*

Albert Bigelow Paine, a poet and author of children's books, approached Clemens about writing his biography shortly after meeting the author in 1901; by 1906, Paine was immersed in Clemens's personal papers and taking dictation from the aging author. Over time, the two men became close friends as Clemens poured forth more than half a million words of what he called "speaking from the grave."

All his life, Clemens juggled the shifting notions of lies and truth. In his autobiography—which, with only an occasional caution, he was giving to his authorized biographer as primary material—he planned to write the truest book ever written. It is a "true" book, in the sense that he poured into it his deflected angers and heterodoxies. He had said that only the dead have free speech. Speaking "as from the grave," he could tell "the truth" about some of the people he had known; he could dictate passages about God and religion which he was sure would get his heirs and assigns burned at the stake if they dared take them out of his box of "posthumous stuff" and publish them before 2006 A.D. But this was only one kind of truth. "You are dramatic and unconscious," Howells wrote to him, "you count the thing more than yourself." Clemens too acknowledged tacitly that introspection and self-analysis were not his strong suit. The truth about *himself* might have to be deduced from his own inevitable lies, evasions, and (as with the letters that Paine was not allowed to read without supervision) reticences. "The remorseless truth *is* there, between the lines," he assured Howells, "where the author-cat is raking dust upon it which hides from the disinterested spectator neither it nor its smell." But by this time Mark Twain was too scarred an author-cat, and also too habituated a storyteller and performer, to give the spectator much of a chance at the truth. Even the vein of self-accusation which runs through the autobiography, and which he regarded as sure proof that he was baring his soul, is in part dramatic rationalizing. Self-accusation was one of his bulwarks against chaos, an act of obedience to the laws of an official and historical identity, Mark Twain, whose authorized biography Clemens himself, long before Paine, had been writing for years.

Only a few weeks after they began working together, Paine realized that Clemens' spellbinding reminiscences "bore only an atmospheric relation to history." He could recall something that had happened only the day before with absolute conviction but with all the essential circumstances turned around, and when Paine reminded him what the facts really were his face took on a blank look, as if he had just waked up. "When I was younger I could remember anything, whether it happened or not," he said to Paine, "but I am getting old, and soon I shall remember only the latter." The question of "whether it happened" is not much more relevant to certain parts of the autobiography than it is to *Huckleberry Finn*. But throughout this chronicle is the talk, the like of which, Howells said, we shall never know again—and we never have. As a record of magnificent talk, magical, hilarious, savage, and tender, the autobiography is a major work, Mark Twain's last, a sprawling and shapeless masterpiece whose unity is in the accent and rhythm and attack of his voice.

In the fifty-four years since his first sketch was published, Mark Twain had written novels, travel books, short stories, essays, plays, plain and fancy journalism. Formal construction baffled him; he wrestled constantly with the problem of point of view, solved it often by writing in the first person, sometimes had to give up altogether. For a while after Susy's death he could finish nothing and was afraid that he could no longer write at all. But in the autobiographical dictations he discovered an anti-form which allowed him a perfect and joyous freedom. "What a dewy and breezy and woodsy freshness it has," he exclaimed to Howells. He might have been speaking from Eden the day talk was invented. Each morning he took up whatever subject interested him and developed it whatever its logical or chronological direction might be; his method was associative, naturalistic, random; in a week's work humor, diatribe, and nostalgia would be all mixed together. In the afternoon he went over the typescript of the morning's dictation and polished it, but he was careful not to eliminate the slips and halts and stumbles which added up, he said, to "the subtle something which makes good talk so much better than the best imitation of it that can be done with a pen." There were drawbacks, of course, when others than Paine and the stenographer were exposed to the method. "Poor man," William James wrote to his brother Henry after dinner with Clemens in February 1907, "only good for monologue, in his old age, or dialogue at best, but he's a dear little genius all the same." James could have saved his pity, because for two and a half years Clemens, spinning out his wild and wonderful history, lived in a creative ecstasy of talking, talking, talking.

He lay in bed and talked, smoking, clenching his fist, pointing with his index finger. When he paused and waited for the word to come he folded the sleeve of his robe or cocked his head at an angle and looked about him. At Dublin, New Hampshire, where he rented a summer house, he paced the long veranda or, when it stormed, the living room, talking all the while. "When I think of that time," Paine wrote, "I shall always hear the ceaseless, slippered, shuffling walk, and see the white figure with its rocking, rolling movement passing up and down the long gallery." And Clemens continued his dictation until the summer of 1908, when he moved into his new house at Redding, discharged his stenographer, and entered, he said, "upon a holiday whose other end is in the cemetery." That year he stopped keeping even the little engagement books that had been serving him for his notes. The last entry he made was the single word, "*Talk.*"

There has never been a time in the past thirty-five years when my literary shipyard hadn't two or more half-finished ships on the way, neglected and baking in the sun; generally there have been three or four; at present there are five. This has an unbusiness-like look but it was not purposeless, it was intentional. As long as a book would write itself I was a faithful and interested amanuensis and my industry did not flag, but the minute that the book tried to shift to my head the labor of contriving its situations, inventing its adventures and conducting its conversations, I put it away and dropped it out of my mind. Then I examined my unfinished properties to see if among them there might not be one whose interest in itself had revived through a couple of years' restful idleness and was ready to take me on again as amanuensis.

It was by accident that I found out that a book is pretty sure to get tired along about the middle and refuse to go on with its work until its powers and its interest should have been refreshed by a rest and its depleted stock of raw materials reinforced by lapse of time. It was when I had reached the middle of Tom Sawyer *that I made this invaluable find. At page 400 of my manuscript the story made a sudden and determined halt and refused to proceed another step. Day after day it still refused. I was disappointed, distressed and immeasurably astonished, for I knew quite well that the tale was not finished and I could not understand why I was not able to go on with it. The reason was very simple—my tank had run dry; it was empty; the stock of materials in it was exhausted; the story could not go on without materials; it could not be wrought out of nothing.*

When the manuscript had lain in a pigeonhole two years I took it out one day and read the last chapter that I had written. It was then that I made the great discovery that when the tank runs dry you've only to leave it alone and it will fill up again in time, while you are asleep—also while you are at work at other things and are quite unaware that this unconscious and profitable cerebration is going on. There was plenty of material now and the book went on and finished itself without any trouble.

Ever since then, when I have been writing a book I have pigeon-holed it without misgivings when its tank ran dry, well knowing that it would fill up again without any of my help. . . .

from The Autobiography of Mark Twain, *edited by* Charles Neider

STORMFIELD

FROM *MR. CLEMENS AND MARK TWAIN*, BY JUSTIN KAPLAN

Livy Clemens died in Florence, Italy, in 1904, after years of illness. She was buried with her son, Langdon, and her daughter, Susy, at the Woodlawn Cemetery in Elmira, New York. Five years later, Clemens lost his youngest daughter Jean, who had been living with him at Stormfield. Jean's sudden death from epilepsy took an enormous toll on Clemens, who wrote an essay he called "The Death of Jean" in memory of his daughter and then vowed, upon completion of that essay, that he would never write again. Above, Stormfield. Photo The Mark Twain House. Below right, Clemens with Jean at Stormfield. Photo courtesy The Mark Twain House.

I lost Susy thirteen years ago; I lost her mother—her incomparable mother!—five and a half years ago; Clara has gone away to live in Europe; and now I have lost Jean. How poor am I, who once was so rich! Seven months ago Mr. Rogers died—one of the best friends I ever had, and the nearest perfect, as a man and gentleman, I have yet met among my race; within the last six weeks Gilder has passed away, and Laffan—old, old friends of mine. Jean lies yonder, I sit here; we are strangers under our own roof; we kissed hands good-by at this door last night— and it was forever, we never suspecting it. She lies there, and I sit here—writing, busying myself, to keep my heart from breaking. How dazzlingly the sunshine is flooding the hills around! It is like a mockery. Seventy-four years old, twenty-four days ago. Seventy-four years old yesterday. Who can estimate my age to-day?

Mark Twain, from "The Death of Jean"

Clemens bought the land for his last home in Redding, Connecticut, sight unseen, and left the design and furnishing of the home up to others. He first laid eyes upon the house the day he moved in, and although he intended to live there only during the summer, he decided immediately that it would be his year-round home. The house took its name from the story "Captain Stormfield's Visit to Heaven," the publication of which helped pay construction costs.

"The country home I need is a cemetery," Clemens had grumbled when the house at Redding was built. But when the house was ready for him he was in the mood for a holiday. At the end of his first day there, in June 1908, he played billiards with Paine until midnight, and during the weeks and months that followed he played endless billiards and games of hearts, walked, went for rides around the countryside. . . . Occasionally, Clemens came out of his retirement. In November he gave a performance—"the same old string of yarns"—for the benefit of the free library he presented to the town. "Poor fellow," Howells said, declining his invitation, "I thought you went to Redding to get rid of Mark Twain." And even though Clemens had begun the vacation he felt sixty years of work had earned him, he still spent his mornings writing in bed. He was busy with letters, his Shakespeare book, and *Letters from the Earth.* In 1909, for *Harper's Bazaar,* he wrote "The Turning-Point of My Life": reviewing his life and legend once again, he saw everything he had done and become as predetermined from the beginning of time, each event only another link in a chain forged by "circumstance, working in harness with my temperament"—he was still pushing away the heavy burden of his freedom. He had discharged his stenographer, but he had not finished his autobiography. He even hit on a new scheme: to write it in the form of letters to friends, letters he would never mail. More than ever he seemed to live in the past and among great expanses of space and time which he figured in light-years. "My father died on this day 63 years ago," he wrote to Clara on March 24, 1910, less than a month before his own death. "I remember all about it quite clearly." He remembered standing in the pilothouse in 1858 and reading a newspaper by the white spray of light of Donati's comet. He had come in with Halley's comet in 1835. In the fall of 1909 the

returning voyager was visible again, at first as a faint nebulous star not far from Orion. "Here are those unaccountable freaks," he imagined God to be saying about Halley's comet and Mark Twain. "They came in together, they must go out together." And he added, "Oh! I am looking forward to that." Like his Connecticut Yankee, he was "getting up his last effect": he was to die at sunset on April 21, one day after the comet reached its perihelion.

A POTENT PRESENCE

FROM *MY MARK TWAIN*, BY WILLIAM DEAN HOWELLS

William Dean Howells lived in Boston, wrote novels and literary criticism, and served as an editor for the respected ATLANTIC MONTHLY *magazine. Shortly after Clemens's death, Howells published the book,* MY MARK TWAIN, *as a final tribute to his friend.*

There is an incident of this time so characteristic of both men that I will yield to the temptation of giving it here. After I had gone to Hartford in response to Clemens's telegram, Matthew Arnold arrived in Boston, and one of my family called on his, to explain why I was not at home to receive his introduction: I had gone to see Mark Twain. "Oh, but he doesn't like *that* sort of thing, does he?" "He likes Mr. Clemens very much," my representative answered, "and he thinks him one of the greatest men he ever knew." I was still Clemens's guest at Hartford when Arnold came there to lecture, and one night we went to meet him at a reception. While his hand laxly held mine in greeting, I saw his eyes fixed intensely on the other side of the room. "Who—who in the world is that?" I looked and said, "Oh, that is Mark Twain." I do not remember just how their instant encounter was contrived by Arnold's wish, but I have the impression that they were not parted for long during the evening, and the next night Arnold, as if still under the glamour of that potent presence, was at Clemens's house. I cannot say how they got on, or what they made of each other; if Clemens ever spoke of Arnold, I do not recall what he said, but Arnold had shown a sense of him from which the incredulous sniff of the polite world, now so universally exploded, had already perished. It might well have done so with his first dramatic vision of that prodigious head. Clemens was then hard upon fifty, and he had kept, as he did to the end, the slender figure of his youth, but the ashes of the burnt-out years were beginning to grey the fires of that splendid shock of red hair which he held to the height of a stature apparently greater than it was, and tilted from side to side in his undulating walk. He glimmered at you from the narrow slits of fine blue-greenish eyes, under branching brows, which with age grew more and more like a sort of plumage, and he was apt to smile into your face with a subtle but amiable perception, and yet with a sort of remote absence; you were all there for him, but he was not all there for you.

William Dean Howells and Samuel Clemens had a great deal in common. Both were born in the Midwest and both began their working lives as printers. Both men tragically lost a daughter at a young age, and both were among the leading literary figures of their day. Not surprisingly, the two men developed an intimate friendship, one which spanned four decades and produced volumes of correspondence. Howells was the first of the literary elite to recognize Clemens's gift as a writer, and he remained Clemens's most ardent supporter. Above, Clemens at Stormfield in the year of his death. Photo The Mark Twain House.

Mark Twain Is Dead

FROM THE *NEW YORK AMERICAN*, APRIL 22, 1910

1905

MT is honored in New York City with a lavish seventieth birthday party.

1906

MT twice addresses Congress on copyright laws.

1906

The United States experiences the worst race riots in its history in the Southern city of Atlanta.

1906

A. B. Paine moves into MT's apartment to begin work on his biography.

1907

MT travels to England for the last time to receive an honorary degree from Oxford University.

1908

MT moves into his final home, which he calls Stormfield, in Redding, Connecticut.

1909

MT's friend Henry H. Rogers dies in May.

1909

The National Association for the Advancement of Colored People is founded.

1909

Explorer Robert Peary reaches the North Pole with his servant Matt Henson and four Eskimo guides.

1909

MT delivers his last public address at a Baltimore school in June.

1909

Jean Clemens, MT's youngest child, dies at Stormfield on Christmas Eve.

1910

Halley's comet returns for the first time since 1835.

1910

Mark Twain dies at Stormfield on April 21.

On the afternoon of Thursday, April 21, 1910, Samuel Clemens slipped into a coma; at sunset, he died. His life had spanned seventy-four years, four months, and three weeks. Only weeks earlier, the author had written to his daughter Clara that he hoped to "go out with Halley's comet," which was at the time visible in the night sky.

MARK TWAIN IS DEAD. It would be hard to frame four other words that could carry a message of personal bereavement to so many Americans. He was easily the chief of our writers, by the only valid test. He could touch the emotional centre of more lives than any other. He was curiously and intimately American. No other author has such a tang of the soil—such a flavor of the average national mind. Europeans who complain that we denied Walt Whitman, misunderstood Emerson and have admired only those who write in old world fashions should be satisfied at least with Mark Twain, and with out unwavering taste for him. He was our very own, and we gathered him to our hearts.

In ages to come, if historians and archaeologists would know the thoughts, the temper, the characteristic psychology of the American of the latter half of the nineteenth century, he will need only to read "Innocents Abroad," "Tom Sawyer," and "Huckleberry Finn." Mr. Clemens's books were the transcripts of his life. And that life was the kind of life that the average American man of his time has believed in and admired. He was the man that rose from the ranks without envy or condescension. The man that hated dogmas and philosophies and loved a flash of intellectual light. He was the man that cared much to get rich, yet would sweat blood to pay his debts. The man of boundless optimism, who has never troubled to understand the great tragedies of nations.

The deepening sense of the twentieth century—with its feeling that there are social problems that cannot be resolved by pleasantries—has somehow left our dear prophet, with all his delicate and tender ironies and his merry quips, a little in the rear. Mark Twain was never fortunate in his polemics. He was not effective as the champion of a cause. . . . He had no natural acerbity, and consequently no real talent for satire. His genius was full of bravery and brightness and the joy of life. And in the strength of his serene and laughing spirit generations of Americans will go forth to do deeds that he himself could never have conceived.

At a funeral held in New York City, Clemens's body was dressed in the white suit that would become his trademark after death. His body was laid to rest in Elmira, New York, at the Woodlawn Cemetery, alongside his wife, his son, and two of his three daughters. Right, Clemens in 1903. Photo the Library of Congress.

A Sage and a Seer

FROM *Mark Twain and His World*, BY JUSTIN KAPLAN

The legacy of Samuel Clemens—of Mark Twain—has proven to be lasting and endlessly compelling. His works have found a permanent place among the classics of modern literature, and his life has never ceased to fascinate students of American history and culture. In this excerpt from Mark Twain and His World, *Justin Kaplan equates the passing of Samuel Clemens with the end of an American era.*

Two currents flowed through Mark Twain's life. One flowed outward and away from the river town of Hannibal, Missouri, toward the nation and the world; the other flowed back home again. Hannibal was the scene of his boyhood, but it remained one of the principal dwelling places of his imagination. Out of the opposition of these currents came a legendary life and a dazzling presence, one of the shaping styles of America's literature and thought, half a dozen of its major books, and such a range of enterprise and concern that in the end Mark Twain is more imposing than the sum of his work. He eludes definitions and categories. He was "sole, incomparable," his friend William Dean Howells said, unlike all the other "literary men" Howells had known. Mark Twain brought to the occupation of humorist a greater profundity, power, and artistry than it had ever had in his country. But "humorist" is not enough to describe him, especially since his own experience demonstrated that in America "humorist" tended to imply the adjective "mere," and the synonym "buffoon." "Author" is too bland; "man of letters" suggests precisely what his vernacular impulses rejected; "novelist" describes only a part of his achievement. Social and political criticism runs through his entire career, from *The Gilded Age* on, but such criticism was the distinctive concern of his old age, when he was also occupied with that anomalous and sprawling masterpiece, his autobiography.

"Sole, incomparable." Those are the words chosen by William Dean Howells to remember his dear friend Samuel Clemens. His esteem for Clemens was a true reflection of public opinion of the time, and of sentiments that remain strong to this day. Nearly a century after his death, the words and images of Mark Twain remain a defining part of the national culture, and his novels remain treasured as American masterpieces— the most American, perhaps, of any literature. Above, Clemens relaxes in his preferred manner, at the billiard table. Photo The Mark Twain House.

In his life he had seen so much and comprehended so much that when he died in 1910 America said goodbye to one of its authentic sages and seers and also to its own young manhood as a nation.

Clemens regarded the honorary degree conferred upon him by England's Oxford University as among the greatest honors of his life. Although he had once sworn never to return to England, he lifted the self-imposed travel ban to accept the degree in 1907. Above, Clemens in England during his visit to Oxford. Photo The Mark Twain House.

Next I saw him dead, lying in his coffin amid those flowers with which we garland our despair in that pitiless hour. After the voice of his old friend Twichell had been lifted in the prayer which it wailed through in broken-hearted supplication, I looked a moment at the face I knew so well; and it was patent with the patience I had so often seen in it; something of puzzle, a great silent dignity, an assent to what must be from the depths of a nature whose tragical seriousness broke in the laughter which the unwise took for the whole of him. Emerson, Longfellow, Lowell, Holmes—I knew them all and all the rest of our sages, poets, seers, critics, humorists; they were like one another and like other literary men; but Clemens was sole, incomparable, the Lincoln of our literature.

from My Mark Twain *by William Dean Howells*

BOOKS BY MARK TWAIN

L isted below, in chronological order, are the major works of Mark Twain published during Samuel Clemens's lifetime. Most are available in several different editions and can be readily located at bookstores and libraries.

THE CELEBRATED JUMPING FROG OF CALAVERAS COUNTY AND OTHER SKETCHES. 1867.

THE INNOCENTS ABROAD, OR THE NEW PILGRIM'S PROGRESS; BEING SOME ACCOUNT OF THE STEAMSHIP QUAKER CITY'S PLEASURE EXCURSION TO EUROPE AND THE HOLY LAND. 1869.

ROUGHING IT. 1872.

THE GILDED AGE: A TALE OF TODAY (CO-AUTHOR CHARLES DUDLEY WARNER). 1874.

THE ADVENTURES OF TOM SAWYER. 1876.

A TRAMP ABROAD. 1880.

THE PRINCE AND THE PAUPER. 1881.

LIFE ON THE MISSISSIPPI. 1883.

ADVENTURES OF HUCKLEBERRY FINN. 1885.

A CONNECTICUT YANKEE IN KING ARTHUR'S COURT. 1889.

THE AMERICAN CLAIMANT. 1892.

MERRY TALES. 1892.

THE £1,000,000 BANK NOTE AND OTHER NEW STORIES. 1893.

TOM SAWYER ABROAD. 1894.

PUDD'NHEAD WILSON AND THOSE EXTRAORDINARY TWINS. 1894.

SKETCHES, NEW AND OLD. 1895.

PERSONAL RECOLLECTIONS OF JOAN OF ARC. 1896.

FOLLOWING THE EQUATOR: A JOURNEY AROUND THE WORLD. 1897.

THE MAN THAT CORRUPTED HADLEYBURG AND OTHER STORIES AND ESSAYS. 1900.

A DOG'S TALE. 1901.

EXTRACTS FROM ADAM'S DIARY. 1904.

EVE'S DIARY. 1906.

WHAT IS MAN? 1906.

THE $30,000 BEQUEST AND OTHER STORIES. 1906.

TRACKING MARK TWAIN

MISSOURI

Mark Twain's Boyhood Home, Hannibal, Missouri. Clemens lived in this house from the end of 1843 until the middle of 1853. This two-story wood-frame house inspired the fictional home of Tom Sawyer. The home has been restored and is preserved as a museum devoted to the life, work, and times of Samuel Clemens.
(573-221-9010)

Pilaster House, Hannibal, Missouri. The Clemens family lived in this house briefly during the 1840s, sharing the accommodations with the doctor who ran a drug store on the first level. Clemens's father died in the house; shortly thereafter his family returned to their house on Hill Street. Today, the house is preserved as a museum run by the Mark Twain Home Foundation.
(573-221-9010)

Becky Thatcher House, Hannibal, Missouri. Located on Hill Street, across from Clemens's boyhood home, this house was home to Laura Hawkins, upon whom Clemens based the character of Becky Thatcher in THE ADVENTURES OF TOM SAWYER. Preserved as a museum, the home has a souvenir and book shop on its first level, while the second story is preserved as it appeared during Clemens's time in Hannibal.
(573-221-9010)

Mark Twain State Park, near Florida, Missouri. A recreational area open to the public for camping, boating, and fishing, this park also contains the Mark Twain Birthplace State Historic Site, where the house in which Clemens was born is preserved as a small museum.
(573-565-3440)

Mark Twain Cave, near Hannibal, Missouri. Since the 1920s, a Missouri family has offered tours of this cave near Hannibal, which has traditionally been identified as the inspiration for the cave in Mark Twain's THE ADVENTURES OF TOM SAWYER. The cave has been designated a natural landmark by the National Park Service.
(573-221-1656)

HARTFORD, CONNECTICUT

The Mark Twain House. The house where Clemens lived for nearly two decades with his wife and children is preserved as a fascinating memorial to Clemens, his works, and his era. The house, a National Register Historic Landmark, is both a public museum and a research facility for Twain scholars.
(860-493-6411)

ELMIRA, NEW YORK

The Center for Mark Twain Studies, Elmira College. The center is located at the site of Quarry Farm, which was owned by Clemens's sister-in-law and her family and was a favorite summer retreat for Clemens and his family.
(607-735-1941)

SONORA, CALIFORNIA

The Mark Twain Cabin. Seven miles from the town of Sonora is a replica of the cabin in which Clemens lived while he wrote "The Celebrated Jumping Frog of Calaveras County."
(209-533-4420)

INDEX

Page numbers in *italic* type refer to photographs and illustrations.